D0979928

MUSIC MARKETING

PRESS, PROMOTION, DISTRIBUTION, AND RETAIL

MIKE KING

Edited by Jonathan Feist

Berklee Press

Vice President: David Kusek
Dean of Continuing Education: Debbie Cavalier
Chief Operating Officer: Robert F. Green
Managing Editor: Jonathan Feist
Editorial Assistants: Yousun Choi, Emily Goldstein, Rajasri Mallikarjuna, Claudia Obser
Cover Designer/Illustrator: Kathy Kikkert

ISBN: 978-0-87639-098-6

1140 Boylston Street
Boston, MA 02215-3693 USA
(617) 747-2146

Visit Berklee Press Online at
www.berkleepress.com

DISTRIBUTED BY

HAL•LEONARD®
CORPORATION
7777 W. BLUEMOUND RD. P.O. BOX 13819
MILWAUKEE, WISCONSIN 53213

Visit Hal Leonard Online at
www.halleonard.com

Contents

ACKNOWLEDGMENTS   vi

PREFACE   viii

**PART ONE SETTING THE STAGE, MERCHANDISING,
DIGITAL AND PHYSICAL RETAIL AND
DISTRIBUTION, AND ONLINE MARKETING   1**

CHAPTER 1   Creating a Marketing Plan That Works   3
            The Big Picture   3
            Defining Your Goals   4
            Finding Your Audience and Defining Your Market   5
            Interview: Dave Balter, Founder of BzzAgent   7
            Components of an Effective Marketing Plan   9
            Budgeting! The Components of a New Release Budget   16
            Tailoring Your Plan to Your Strengths   17

CHAPTER 2   Making Money through Merchandise Sales   19
            The Artist as a Brand   19
            How Merchandising Works, Who's Involved, and
                Where the Money Comes From   21
            Putting Together Your Plan: What to Make, What Not
                to Make, How Much to Make, How to Make It   23
            Merchandising Sales and Distribution Strategies   28

CHAPTER 3   How to Sell Your Music Online:
            Digital Retailers and Distributors   33
            Digital Distribution Basics   33
            Online Music Retail Models   38
            Online Music Retail Outlets   40
            Interview: Bob Jamieson, Former CEO of RCA/BMG   44
            Online Music Distributors   46
            Interview: Derek Sivers, Founder of CD Baby   50

CHAPTER 4   Traditional Brick-and-Mortar Distributors   59
            Physical Music Distributors: The Process and the Players   59
            When Do You Need Physical Distribution?   62
            Independent Artists and Distribution   63
            Spotlight: Eric Levin (Criminal Records)   63
            The Details   64
            Co-Op   66
            Communicating with Your Distributor   69

CHAPTER 5   Marketing to Traditional Retail   73
            Setting the Stage: The Problems with Retail, and
                How Smart Stores Are Overcoming Them   73
            The Importance of the Independent Retailer and
                Retail Coalitions   76
            Interview: Eric Levin, Founder of Criminal Records   78
            How Smart Independents Are Competing in
                This Environment   78
            Consignment and Pricing Considerations   80
            Retail Marketing Opportunities and Resources   80
            Cover Art and Effective Packaging   82
            SoundScan: What It Is and Why It Matters   84

CHAPTER 6   Online, Mobile, and Video Marketing   87
            It All Starts at Home   87
            SEO: Making Your Site POP!   93
            Measuring Your Online Traffic and Marketing Results   96
            What Is RSS and Why Should I Use It?   98
            Social Networking   99
            The Mobile Revolution   102
            Video Marketing   104

PART TWO ADVERTISING CONSIDERATIONS,
            MARKETING TO PRESS AND RADIO,
            AND MAKING THE MOST OF YOUR
            NATIONAL TOUR   109

CHAPTER 7   Advertising   111
            Print Advertising Options: Consumer, Trade, and
                Co-Op Print Ads   112
            Researching Your Print Advertising Outlets   115
            Media Advertising: Radio and Television   117
            Online Advertising   118
            Components of an Effective Ad   121
            Timing Your Ad Campaign   123

CHAPTER 8	Publicity	127
	Press Kit Essentials	127
	Common Problems with Promo Kits	132
	The Importance of a Press Story	133
	Determining Your Press Outlets: Print, Radio, TV, and Online	136
	How to Pitch Print Media	139
	Independent Publicists	141
	Interview: Sonya Kolowrat, Publicist for the Beggars Group	146
CHAPTER 9	**Radio Promotion**	**151**
	How Radio Works	151
	When Should You Consider Radio Support?	152
	How a Terrestrial (Brick-and-Mortar) Radio Station Is Structured	153
	How Noncommercial Radio Works	154
	Marketing to Noncommercial Radio	156
	How Commercial Radio Works	157
	Independent Radio Promoters	160
	Internet Radio: The Future of Radio	163
	Interview: Bob Jamieson, Former CEO of RCA/BMG	166
CHAPTER 10	**Making the Most of a Tour**	**169**
	Key Players in the Touring Business	170
	Interview: Dan Peraino, Booking Agent	172
	Promoting the Show: Working with the Venue	175
	Promoting the Show: What You Should Be Doing to Promote Yourself	176
	Promoting the Show: Press	177
	Promoting the Show: Retail	179
	Tour Support from a Label	182
PART THREE	**PUTTING IT ALL TOGETHER**	**185**
CHAPTER 11	**Timing Is Everything!**	**187**
	Timing the Pre-Release Marketing of Your Record	187
	Long Lead Pre-Release Marketing (15 to 20 Weeks out from Street Date)	190
	Moderate Lead Pre-Release Marketing (7 to 14 Weeks out from Street Date)	191
	Short Lead Pre-Release Marketing (Up to 6 Weeks Out)	192
	How to Service Key Marketing Outlets Pre-Release	193
	Post-Release Marketing Recap	195
	Phase II Marketing: Capitalizing on Your Success	198
CONCLUSION		**203**
ABOUT THE AUTHOR		**205**
INDEX		**206**

Acknowledgments

Thanks to Dave Kusek, Debbie Cavalier, and Don Gorder for the opportunity; Jill Christiansen for the hands-on education; George Howard; John Snyder; Jonathan Feist for an expert editing job and excellent ideas, and Charlotte Finlay for teaching me to listen. Additional thanks to Ewald Christians from TuneCore.com.

Extra special thanks to the industry experts that agreed to do an interview with me: Dave Balter, Bob Jamieson, Derek Sivers, Eric Levin, Brandon Bosh, Sonya Kolowrat, and Dan Peraino.

For Nicci and my parents, Robert, and Bonnie King: Thank you for your unending support and encouragement.

Preface

It's a great time to be involved in music marketing!

The music industry is shifting, the traditional gatekeepers are evolving (or disappearing), and new marketing outlets are popping up all the time. While this might mean some uncomfortable changes to some of the traditional marketing outlets that labels and independents have focused on for years, it also brings a *huge* amount of opportunity and fresh outlets for marketing folks.

The key to a successful music marketing campaign is a completely integrated, highly targeted, and effectively timed campaign that takes advantages of the traditional outlets that still matter, as well as the new technologies, distribution methods, and marketing techniques that the Internet has brought us.

The goal of this book is to provide artists, managers, indie label owners, and music industry entrepreneurs with a detailed music marketing roadmap—one that mixes high-concept marketing techniques with concrete practical in-the-field suggestions. Throughout this book, we'll discuss all the segments that work towards creating an effective worldwide marketing strategy: publicity, radio, retail and distribution, merchandising, online marketing, advertising, and touring. You'll learn what players are involved at the highest levels of music marketing, how to communicate with them, and ways to leverage the changes and new opportunities that the digital music community offers to marketers. You'll also learn to how to wrap all this content together in a perfectly timed marketing plan that can be immediately implemented into your existing marketing and promotion campaigns.

The digital revolution has enabled any musician to record and distribute their music with relative ease. The new challenge for musicians is in finding ways to differentiate themselves from the crowd, and develop engaging ways to communicate with their potential fans. The information in this book will give you the tools to develop a voice that can be heard over the rest. Let's get started!

PART

ONE

Setting the Stage, Merchandising, Digital and Physical Retail and Distribution, and Online Marketing

1

Creating a Marketing Plan That Works

Every so often, a band or artist comes around that is absolutely everywhere. You read about them online, you hear them being played in your local indie record store, they appear in your Pandora playlist, they're profiled in *Paste* or *Rolling Stone*, they are being interviewed on *Morning Becomes Eclectic* on KCRW, and your hip coworkers have added them to their shared iTunes playlist. This doesn't just "happen." This is actually a sign that someone, somewhere, has done a great job building an *integrated music marketing* campaign for this artist.

Integrated music marketing is a concept where all aspects of a particular artist's campaign, including touring, merchandising, press, radio, retail/distribution, Internet/mobile, video, and any ancillary marketing, (such as licensing placements, advertising or other outreach) work together as a unified force to build visibility, rather than working on their own in isolation.

Creating a critical mass, or "tipping point"—where the momentum of a project becomes self-sustaining—is the end goal of all marketers. Throughout this book, we'll be talking about all the tools and techniques that artists (or folks responsible for artists' careers, like managers and music industry entrepreneurs) should consider when developing a living, working, active music marketing plan designed to help create a critical mass— one that is tailored to the artist's own strengths.

While all artists' goals are different and not all marketing segments should be a consideration for all artists all the time, it's important to have an understanding of the complete range of possibilities. (Who knows what might change for you in the future!) In this chapter, we'll look at an overview of the primary marketing areas all artists should consider, and how to organize these separate marketing segments into a cohesive plan that can be used to guide the overall marketing efforts.

THE BIG PICTURE

A marketing plan is a fluid, living guide to help you focus all of your marketing efforts towards a single goal. No two are alike (well, they shouldn't be). They take into account the strengths and weaknesses of you or your band, and the innovations and new developments that are constantly popping up in the music industry. Marketing plans are useful for putting your thoughts to paper, and in helping you to allocate your time and resources towards a predetermined "path to success." All labels have marketing plans for their artists (if you get signed, you should always ask to see yours), and all enterprising unsigned artists or artist managers should have a working marketing plan as well.

DEFINING YOUR GOALS

The first thing you have to think about when putting together your marketing plan is this: What is your core goal? Is your goal to use this release to get a label deal? Is your goal to sell 20,000 records in a year yourself, from the stage? Is your goal to break out from Liverpool, play some shows in Hamburg, and become the biggest band in the world? It's essential for marketers to realize that the most successful and long-lasting campaigns start locally and build globally, and that no matter how grand the overall goal is, it makes sense for all artists to attack this goal on a per-project basis. A typical music marketing plans looks at the lifecycle of one record (which could end up being more than a year for a well-performing release).

For traditional record labels, the goal was easy: sell records. Labels have the infrastructure in place (distribution and marketing, mostly) to replicate past marketing plans with slight adjustments based on the individual characteristics and existing fan base of the particular band they are working. Independent artists that do not have a label's built-in promotion and distribution mechanisms must be more detailed with their plans. For example, a band with a small hometown following might have the core goal of using their new release to expand their fan base. A band that was formerly signed to a label might be interested in tapping into the national or international marketing inroads that their former label made. This plan might have the goal of connecting with past supporters of the band to sell an independent release.

Reality Check

It's essential to have a long-term vision of being "the toppermost of the poppermost!" as John Lennon used to say, but in terms of creating a working marketing plan, you need to consider the stage you are at in your career and be realistic about what is possible for you.

FINDING YOUR AUDIENCE AND DEFINING YOUR MARKET

Probably the most crucial aspect of any music marketing campaign is to determine who your core audience is. For a marketing plan to be effective (especially for a developing artist), all your efforts need to target your primary customer—your fan—as directly as possible. Marketing is expensive and time-consuming. There is nothing worse than implementing an outreach plan and finding that you are talking to the wrong people! Spending time researching who your potential fans are, where they hang out, how old they are, how they get their music information, and how they buy music will dictate what marketing specific avenues you pursue in the rest of your marketing plan.

Artists need to focus in on and be aware of a number of things in order to effectively laser in on their target audience. You must:

Narrow your scope. It's not uncommon for a developing band to want to be all things to all people. One of the defining moments for me at Ryko was when we were pitched by a band's manager to sign a new band he was working with out of New York City. We saw the band play live, and they were as far as you can get from being tight performers. The players were an odd mix from all sorts of styles: a female jazz singer was mixed with an old blues singer, a shredding guitar player, conga player, and a Bootsy Collins–imitator bassist. The songs they played were equally diverse. We caught up with the manager after the show, and let him know that the project wasn't for us; it would be impossible to market. He responded, "What do you mean? This band has everything! You can market to everybody!"

Folks need a point of reference that they can identify with. If a band is all over the place in genres, it's very difficult to build a following and create the all-important emotional connection with the fans. Don't try to be everything to everybody.

Pick your niche, build a following, then expand your niche as your fan base grows.

Be organized and build on past successes. It's essential to keep the contact info (easily done with programs like FileMaker) of everyone that has helped you throughout your career—writers, radio folks, retailers, promoters, and so on. No matter what stage you're at in your career, your marketing plan should include a list of past supporters in all these marketing areas. Folks within the industry that are fans of your music are key to reconnecting with an existing fan base that you might not have the opportunity to reach otherwise.

Research like-minded artists. Many marketing plans have a section that includes competitive analysis, which requires you to research the audience, branding, and marketing techniques of a similar product. With a music marketing plan, a competing product would be a band that you think shares the same general genre and sound as your own. Researching a band that is further along in their career is a good way to help determine who your audience might be. What kind of Web visibility do they have? What venues are they playing? Are they playing many all-ages shows? What cities are they playing in? SoundScan is useful in determining popular markets and the types of purchases that have been made from these artists (tour sales, retail sales, and digital sales). (See chapter 5 for more about SoundScan.)

Look at who's coming to your shows. It may seem obvious, but the folks that come out to see you play are a small microcosm of the folks you should be targeting in your overall marketing plan. You may be creating your music with mid-twenties hipsters in mind, but if you see that you have high school age kids coming out to see you play, you need to adjust your marketing accordingly. Your audience at shows is absolutely key in helping to determine your broader marketing campaign.

Data mining. In addition to the direct marketing opportunities you have with your e-mail list, the names of the folks that have signed up to keep in touch with your band represent a great cross section of who your market is. Asking some quick demographic questions on the e-mail sign-up sheet (age, address/zip code, and some basic marketing questions like, "Where do you hear about new music?") will help you to better identify your overall potential market.

Unique Selling Proposition. Your *unique selling proposition* is what differentiates your band from the thousands of other artists out there. In many ways, defining your market and finding your niche begins with how you brand and position yourself. Creating a unique selling proposition (USP) goes a long way towards helping you define your target market.

INTERVIEW: DAVE BALTER,
FOUNDER OF BZZAGENT

Reaching a "critical mass" through word of mouth is something that Dave Balter knows a lot about. In 2002, Dave founded BzzAgent, a word-of-mouth media company that currently coordinates volunteer "agents" in the U.S., Canada, and the U.K. Dave recently wrote and self-published his second book on word-of-mouth marketing, creatively titled The Word of Mouth Manual Volume II.

What does BzzAgent do?

BzzAgent is a word-of-mouth media company that connects brands with people to accelerate and sustain the sharing of opinions. We have over 450,000 BzzAgents and have run nearly 500 programs for more than 250 clients.

What is the difference between a word-of-mouth campaign and a viral campaign?

"Word of mouth" is the sharing of an opinion between one or more consumers, and the campaign is focused on enabling consumers to share their opinions effectively in whatever way they're comfortable. "Viral marketing" is the utilization of a marketing tool that gets people to pass a message along to each other. Think the Paris Hilton Carl's Jr. video or the Lance Armstrong bracelet. These tools can sometimes lead to the sharing of an opinion, but often the dialogue is about the tool itself rather than the product.

"Viral marketing"—if it works—is often rapid and explosive, but due to the limited attention of consumers, it can fizzle just as quickly. Word of mouth is often much more steady and constant, as once people form an opinion, they share it freely.

What are some ways that artists can help to inspire a word-of-mouth campaign?

First and foremost, create great music. Nothing beats someone telling someone else that they "have to hear this," or more like, "These guys blew my mind..." In that vein, simplifying how people can hear your music is incredibly important. Think of it as removing as many hurdles to getting to someone's ears as possible.

What are some tools that artists can use to help them in the process?

Giving away free music is always a good starting point: if people don't know what you sound like, they can't tell someone else to listen. Finding creative ways to connect with a listener can be powerful as well, especially if that connection results in a story worth telling. Think of the guy on Venice Beach who roller-skates and plays his guitar. If you run into him, you're never going to forget it. The Grateful Dead are a pure embodiment of word of mouth. With little to no radio airplay (their first Billboard hit came more than twenty years into their career), they built a massive audience who bought their albums and attended their concerts. One reason: they allowed free sharing and taping of their music so that anyone who had an interest didn't have to go far to listen in.

The Dead also realized that impromptu set lists and jamming created a deep connection with the audience. So much so that people treated each show as a special event that they would share with others. The stories of which songs were played in what order were as important as the music itself.

Once a word-of-mouth campaign is happening, what ways can an artist use this momentum to help forward their career?

Never forget that each person has the ability to create listeners out of their social circle—and just as easily can slow your progress. Make every individual feel special (extra backstage passes, buying someone a drink instead of letting them buy you one, playing a song they request), and they'll talk about you forever. In some senses, the music becomes secondary once they've made the decision that they like who you are. That connection becomes the critical element in sustaining their word of mouth to others.

COMPONENTS OF AN EFFECTIVE MARKETING PLAN

Once you have your goals in mind and have defined your market, it's time to put pen to paper (or hands to keyboard) and sketch out a draft outlining exactly how you plan on reaching these goals and attracting the attention of your defined audience.

While a marketing plan is primarily a vehicle for you to use to guide your promotional efforts, keep in mind that other folks are likely going to be reading this as well, especially if you decide to work with outside help. Remember, no marketing segment works in a vacuum. If you decide to work with a publicist, distributor, or radio promo person, these folks are all going to want to see your entire plan to determine where exactly they fit in, and how they can help further your overall goal.

Marketing plans need to focus on the strengths of a particular band. However, there are certain foundational areas that all plans need to address (all of which we will go into more detail on later in the book).

Artist/Album Description

The artist/album description is written for the benefit of the folks that you might be working with to execute your marketing plan. Many of the same elements from your bio (see chapter 8) can be worked in here: how the band started, who the players are, a quote from a press outlet or from the lead spokesperson in the band, where the band has toured and who they have toured with, and any other interesting elements that will help to give folks a point of reference about the band's music and story.

Target Demographic and Geographic Markets

Your target demographic should also be detailed in your marketing plan, based on the research techniques we talked about in "Defining Your Market." What age group would you classify your typical fan in? What other music would they likely listen to? Where do they live? Have you made any headway in particular markets that you should revisit? Where do comparable artists do well? Your target demo and markets will dictate where you focus your marketing dollars and efforts throughout your entire campaign.

Press

Every marketing plan should contain a press component. Whether it's local, regional, online, or national press, publicity is one marketing segment that all artists can make headway in, regardless of budget or what point the artist is at in their career. The press component of the marketing plan should talk about who will be working the record (an independent publicist or in-house person), what kind of press will be the focus (tour press/regional press/major national press/NPR/blogs, etc.), any supporters the band already had in the press world, target writers who have written about similar artists, and very specific target press outlets.

Online/Video

Online marketing is another vital segment that all artists need to address in their plan. What are you doing on your own site to raise awareness? How are you engaging and interacting with your fans? What is the outreach plan you have for your own e-mail list? Are you planning on developing any cool players or viral features to announce the record? Are there any contests you can create to build visibility online? How will you optimize your micro-blogging campaign? Is there any video you can use/create with the goal of starting a viral campaign? What third-party sites can you partner with?

Distribution/Retail

How are you planning on getting your music distributed? Will you be selling off your own site, selling from the stage, working with a digital distributor, or working with a physical distributor? Are you going for a regional or national physical release? Will you be servicing select stores through consignment?

If you are working with physical retailers, it is key to identify target stores in your target markets and outline how you will market to them. Are you creating tour/retail posters? Will you create limited edition homemade 4-track singles? Are you going to make bin cards?

Radio

As we'll discuss in the chapter on radio, traditional terrestrial commercial radio is not for everyone. But it is likely that some form of radio makes sense. Online radio, specialty shows, and noncommercial radio are outlets that many artists can take advantage of in the early stages of their career. Your marketing plan should talk about whether radio is a viable outlet for you, and if so, who will work the project to radio (an indie or in-house person), what radio segment will be worked and when, and any additional opportunities you will be addressing while on tour (phoners, in-studio opportunities, ticket giveaways, etc.).

Tour

Your marketing plan should include an outline of your tour plans—where you are planning to play and when. If the dates aren't firmed up, that's okay. All of the other marketing areas will work off these dates, and an outline of where you intend to play if the dates are not firmed up yet is enough information to get the other segments stirring.

Advertising

Advertising is not a component of all marketing plans. However, if you feel that you would benefit from an ad campaign, an overview of the outlets, the ad sizes, the frequency, and any messaging you want included makes sense.

Promotional Merchandise

Over and above the items you create to sell on your site or at your shows, it makes sense to create specific promotional items particular to promoting your new record. What items will you create to support your tour/retail/radio efforts? Certainly, tour posters make sense to touring artists. Your marketing plan should outline any items you plan on creating.

Additional Opportunities

What other promotional avenues can you take advantage of? Do you organize an annual rock show in your town? Do any of the members in your band play with other bands that might be able to help promote this new record? Do you have any friends in high places that can help you out? Are there any lifestyle opportunities you can take advantage of (friends that work at Urban Outfitters or other stores that cater to your potential audience, that can spin your advance, for example)? What areas outside of the traditional marketing segments can you take advantage of?

SAMPLE MARKETING PLAN: ZAPPA PICKS

This record-release marketing plan was for two Frank Zappa compilations, by Larry LaLonde of Primus and John Fishman from Phish. While some of the outlets no longer exist, this is a good example of the formatting and structure of a record-release marketing plan.

FRANK ZAPPA
ZAPPA PICKS—BY JON FISHMAN OF PHISH
ZAPPA PICKS—BY LARRY LALONDE OF PRIMUS
SALES & MARKETING PLAN

Artist/ Project Overview

"I find this music so wonderful that no matter what I'm listening to, or just finding out about, Frank's music is always on my personal play list, and I never get tired of it. How could you?"—Larry LaLonde (Primus)

"…it is safe to say that the work of Frank Zappa, his music primarily, but also his humor, politics, social commentary…all of it…has not just been a fundamental influence on me, but is actually more like part of my metabolism."—Jon Fishman (Phish)

Frank Zappa played with some of the most skilled and original musicians throughout his almost thirty-year recording career (included among them: Captain Beefheart, Shuggie Otis, Steve Vai, Jean-Luc Ponty, Adrian Belew, Ruth Underwood, John Lennon), and in the process, he and his various bands influenced countless musicians—musicians that would later go on to spread his influence to fans over a very broad musical spectrum. When you hear the Red Hot Chili Peppers guitarist John Frusciante, you are hearing Zappa's influence. Beck, Jaco Pastorius, Primus, and numerous bands within the "improv rock scene" (with Phish being the most notable) have all been influenced by Zappa.

Zappa Picks—By Jon Fishman of Phish, and *Zappa Picks—By Larry LaLonde of Primus* are the first in what will become an ongoing "celebrity" picks series. The goal of these releases, as is the goal for any Zappa release we put out, is to build awareness for the entire Zappa catalog (*more than sixty records*) on Rykodisc. Phish has never been shy to speak about their admiration of Zappa. In *The Phish Book* (written by Richard Gehr, who is writing the press release for this picks series), Trey Anastasio says, "I have the highest respect for Zappa, for who he was, what he represented, and the fact that he didn't give a shit what anybody else thought about him or his music. Zappa pushed his bands to the limit, wrote music that challenged people, and always worked at the edge of his abilities." The Phish and Primus compilations are intended to turn on a group of kids that are rabid music fans. Both bands have a hard-core fan base that fits the perfect mold for a Zappa consumer: eighteen-year-old (male mostly) somewhat disenfranchised outsiders, who identify with the lyrical humor in Primus and Phish songs. These kids also identify with musical virtuosos (Les Claypool, Trey Anastasio). Zappa would certainly bring it on home for them in this department.

The tracks on both compilations are, oddly enough, almost exactly what you think the artists would pick. Jon Fishman chose Zappa compositions that are more guitar-based and tend to really rip musically. Larry LaLonde's picks tend to skew more towards Zappa's "lyrical humor." Both are brilliantly sequenced, and in true Zappa form, there is no space between tracks. Each track segues into the next.

Again, this is a perfect opportunity to reopen a dialogue with retailers, press, radio programmers, music supervisors, and Zappa fanatics.

Best geographic markets for Zappa: Everywhere, but especially New York City, Chicago, Los Angeles, San Francisco, Boston, Philadelphia, Detroit, Washington D.C.

Best geographic markets for Phish: Top SoundScan markets are New York City, Boston, Denver, San Francisco, Chicago, Philadelphia, Los Angeles, Washington D.C.

Best geographic markets for Primus: Top SoundScan markets are New York City, Los Angeles, San Francisco, Chicago, Boston, Philadelphia, Denver, Seattle.

PRESS

L.A.-based indie publicist Cary Baker of Baker/Northrop has been working these projects since late August. Coverage thus far includes:

- Billboard.com
- Rollingstone.com
- MTV.com
- MJI Triple A Daily
- Undercover
- CDNOW
- ABC Radio today
- Jambands.com

Press was reawakened to some new Zappa with the Threesome sets we put out in April. The sets were by and large well received. We got some great reviews in *Spin*, *Blender* (5-star review for "Threesome No. 2"), *Relix*, and regional outlets. We expect to get Jon and Larry interviews/reviews/features about these compilations from traditional Zappa outlets as well as outlets particular to each release. Initial positive response from writers is encouraging.

Zines and college publications will be important for our Zappa press campaign, especially the zines that are anti-establishment/live-free-or-die types (*Punk Planet*, *Clamour*, *Splendid Zine*), and the multitude of online resources. We've also put together a great target list of jam/improv-friendly writers and publications from the work we've done with the Slip and Pork Tornado. The Phish organization has been extremely helpful with supplying us with information on supportive press outlets and writers.

Both Jon and Larry are willing to do interviews. Online live chats will also be explored.

Targets

- National music magazines: *Rolling Stone*, *Spin*, *Magnet*, *Revolver*, *Alternative Press*
- Key/supportive writers in the improv rock scene will be a major focus: Jonathan Cohen (*Billboard*), Steve Morse (*Boston Globe*), Brian Baker (various Midwest regional publications, G. Brown (Denver/Boulder), Hilton Price (regional: west coast)
- Zines: *Big Takeover*, *Amplifier*, *Stop Smiling*, *Rockpile*, *Skyscraper*, *Loud Paper*, *Devil in the Woods*, *Chunklet*, *Baffler*, *Clamour*, *Splendid Zine*
- College papers: Our in-house publicist has put together a database of ninety college papers nationwide.

- Musician magazines like *Guitar Magazine, Guitar Player, Vintage Guitar, Guitar One, Drum!, Modern Drummer*
- National magazines/papers/men's mags: *Entertainment Weekly, Blender, Playboy, Time, USA Today, Maxim, Mother Jones, Utne*
- Collector magazines: *Goldmine, Ice*
- Hippie/Dead–type magazines: *Relix, High Times, Signal To Noise*
- Internet outlets: Jambase.com, Pitchforkmedia.com
- Major dailies/key regionals, with particular focus on Los Angeles, San Francisco, Chicago, New York, Boston, Boulder/Denver

RADIO

In addition to servicing the various "Zappa Hours" on-air around the country, we are making a run at college radio. We are doing a full service to college radio with an ad date of October 8. We are also servicing one-hundred to-be-selected Triple A radio. We may use some of the 4/4 postcards ("rave cards") we are producing at the CMJ festival in October/November.

RETAIL

One of the goals of this "picks" series is to highlight the extensive Zappa catalog on Rykodisc. These releases are perfectly timed for a Zappa Halloween extravaganza/promotions at retail, which we can use to highlight the entire back catalog. We are also putting together a video reel for key retailers, which will feature three or four live video clips (one of which is a live performance of *Stinkfoot*, which we included on our distribution retail in New Orleans). Rave cards will be distributed to supportive retailers as well.

Indie Retail

Top indie stores for Frank Zappa: Newbury Comics/Boston (P&P), Rolling Stone/Chicago (P&P), Bull Moose/NH, Maine (P&P, possible radio tie-in with "Zappa Hour" in Portland, ME), Homers/Nebraska (P&P), Waterloo/Austin (Waterloo recommends), Plan 9/Virginia (9X cut, P&P), Silver Platters/Seattle (Platter Chatter, P&P), Manifest/N. Carolina (P&P), Crows Nest/Chicago (P&P), Music Millennium/Portland (Cut in Willamette Weekly and endcap), Rasputin/Berkeley, CA (endcap).

We will also pay special attention to top jam/groove accounts: Twist and Shout/Denver, Barts/Boulder, Electric Fetus/Minneapolis, Homegrown Music (online), Uncle Bucks/MS.

Chain Stores

Musicland

- Strong supporter of Zappa
- Sending display materials

Best Buy

- Regional focus in NYC, L.A., San Francisco, Chicago, Boston

Transworld

- Will seek endcap programs

Wherehouse

- Regional programs where applicable

Borders

- Supporter of Zappa, we'll send rave cards

Other Targets

- Amazon.com (w/download)
- Barnesandnoble.com
- Borders.com
- Homegrownmusic.com

PHISH AND PRIMUS RESOURCES

Phish and Primus have sent e-mails to their respective lists (Primus is 35k, Phish is 75k) and will again in the coming weeks. We currently have front-page placement on both sites, and both sites will cross promote Rykodisc. Both management companies will purchase the CD from us to sell directly to fans.

We're producing 15,000 "rave cards" (they look like postcards with two color fronts), which Phish will distribute in the following manner:

- Phish mail order will distribute in all the *Vol III Live Phish* series packages that ship out in October.
- Pork Tornado will have the cards available on their six-week tour.
- Strong possibility of distribution on Trey Anastasio fall tour and Phish Madison Square Garden New Year's Eve play.

INTERNET MARKETING

Rykodisc Web feature will be completed by Cal Schenkel. It will include:

- Bio/Press release
- Personal notes from Larry and Jon
- Album info, with thirty-second sound bites of select tracks
- E-mail registration
- Various unusual secrets and surprises
- Link to buy
- Link to FZ main Ryko feature
- Link to Phish.com and Primusucks.com
- Contest page
- Cal Schenkel trademark delights and surprises

MATERIALS

- 2-sided rave cards (4/4 postcard style; two versions, one with Pork Tornado on one side/*Zappa Picks* on the other, the other with the Slip/Pork Tornado on one side and *Zappa Picks* on the other side)

- 24" x 36" retail poster ("Sometimes you can't write a chord ugly enough...")

- 18" x 24" retail poster (Frank on tractor for strictly commercial *The Best Of*)

- 18" x 24" retail poster (Cal Schenkel catalog poster)

BUDGETING! THE COMPONENTS OF A NEW RELEASE BUDGET

Once you have an idea of the outlets, areas, and segments you'll need to target to reach your audience, it's time to take a step back and look at the financial realities of your draft plan. Similar to any major project, a budget needs to go hand in hand with whatever plan you'd like to implement. Your initial plan might include skywriting your band's new record and release date over the New York City skyline, but if the financial numbers for this particular marketing initiative don't work, you're going to have to reconsider.

One of the primary considerations of any budget is to outline something that is designed to keep you (or your label) in the black. The primary revenue sources are not the same as they were five years ago, and it's important to look at what sources of revenue you currently have coming in, and the ones you expect to continue to come in, from touring, merch, licensing, online and physical sales, and so on. It's also vitally important to be realistic! I've seen several projects where the sales numbers were inflated to such a degree that it was no surprise to see that when the marketing campaign was over, the label had spent upwards of $10 per unit on marketing! It's tough to make any money with a marketing spend that high.

A new-release budget should take into account the following:

Expectations

What are your sales goals? What do you realistically think you can sell/ship over a three-month/six-month/twelve-month time frame? How much income will this provide for you? What other income do you expect to come in through merch, touring, licensing, ring tones, or other events?

Marketing costs broken out by segment

Look at every segment you plan to market to, and determine the complete budget you will need to effectively market to this area. If you are using a radio promoter, for example, their fee should go into your budget, along with any trade ads they plan on taking out, promo items they need produced, mailing fees, etc. This needs to happen for every promotional area.

General marketing costs

Do you plan on taking out any online or print ads? Do you need to hire someone to design a Web site for you? Are you going to make counter cards, posters, white label 4-track promos? What are the mailing costs you expect to incur for sending these items out?

Manufacturing costs

Are you going to create promo copies of your CD for press/radio/ retail outreach? If so, the manufacturing of these should be included in your overall marketing budget.

TAILORING YOUR PLAN TO YOUR STRENGTHS

It's not uncommon for developing artists to think that they need to address as many promotional segments as possible when they develop their marketing plan. As we'll discuss in more detail later, there are plenty of indie promoters or publicists out there that have no problem taking money from artists, with the goal of soliciting them to radio or press even when it's not necessarily in the best interest of the project. When creating a music-marketing plan, it's absolutely essential to be as targeted as possible.

Once you've determined your goals, your target audience, and your unique selling proposition, it's important to research the specific marketing vehicles that are most effective in reaching this audience and explaining your story.

As an example, a friend of mine has a project where he and his collaborator remix traditional instruments and songs from countries that traditionally are politically at odds with one another. One of his songs is a wonderful mix of traditional Sufi music from Iran and sea shanties from Basra in Iraq. The goal of his music is to show that even if governments are on the opposite side of the political fence, unity and peace can be achieved through these countries' music. This band does not tour, and will likely never be able to do any live events, as the two main members are corresponding from different countries across the world. In the case of this particular band, traditional retail and radio would not make sense as a first step, as the band would not be able to kick-start the marketing in specific geographic areas through a tour. However, the band is extremely tied in online, and has created several amazing animated videos that are starting to get a good amount of visibility online. The band's Web site is as interactive as you can get, and the band's press story is timely.

In this particular example, the target audience was determined to be educated thirty-plus males and females with a wide world-view. The unique selling proposition was the press story. The marketing plan relied heavily on online marketing, selling from their site, online distribution, and an allotment for press—with the goal of coverage on NPR and the BBC, *Utne Reader*, *The New York Times*, *Mother Jones*, etc. Touring, physical retail, and radio were not considerations for this particular release because of the band's target audience, and the band's lack of a live presence.

Summary

Setting realistic goals, defining your audience, and finding niche markets (playing to your strengths) are all very important aspects to creating a marketing plan that works. While there are specific segments from which a marketing plan always draws from, it's key to understand that all plans are different, and that artists should focus on areas where they feel they can have the most impact. Moreover, having a handle on your budget helps to dictate the proper outlets to target. There is no point in targeting national commercial radio without a national distribution campaign—and a budget to support it! Start slow, build your base, and target outlets that are within reach and will have an immediate and tangible impact on your band's visibility.

Workshop

- Prepare a one-page overview outlining your overall goals, your unique selling proposition, who your core audience is, any past supporters, and what similar artists are doing to market themselves. We'll use this information as the starting point for your marketing plan, which we will revisit throughout the book.

2 Making Money through Merchandise Sales

No matter how large or small your band is, a successful merchandise plan needs to play a part in your marketing. A good merchandise plan accomplishes a couple of things: you create an additional revenue stream that you can tap into for other marketing areas (or gas for your vehicle), and the merchandise you make (with your very visible logo) makes for great advertising that will turn other folks on to your band.

Touring and merchandising go hand in hand. Touring provides the opportunity to get your gear in front of a different group of captive fans every night (as well as the folks whom you have converted through your amazing show), and it also provides an incentive for nimble artists to create limited-edition, tour-branded items that existing fans will also love. The details on what items you should make are certainly dictated by the demographic of your following, your budget limitations, as well as where you are currently at in your career, but overall, every band should have some form of merchandise available for sale at live events and online. Plus, it's not uncommon for fans to pay an average of more than $5 each on merchandise at a show!

THE ARTIST AS A BRAND

There's a lot to be learned from hip-hop marketing.

In many genres, aligning oneself with a product has been considered taboo. Hip-hop, on the other hand, was founded with an entrepreneurial spirit in mind. Russell Simmons, cofounder of Def Jam, and considered "the godfather of hip-hop," shepherded the genre into the American mainstream in the 1980s. Before selling his interest in Def Jam to Universal for a reported $100 million in 1999, Simmons had already produced several films, the groundbreaking HBO series *Russell Simmons' Def Comedy Jam*, a successful men's clothing line, and a hip-hop lifestyle magazine.

In 1982, Simmons took on his younger brother Joseph's group as clients, christened them Run-DMC, and the following year created the first brand deal in rap history with Adidas. Adidas's Run-DMC branded shoes are still available, twenty-five years later!

Modern day hip-hop entrepreneur Jay-Z has continued hip-hop's branding connection with his deals with Budweiser and Reebok. And perhaps most successful at branding in recent years is 50 Cent, who has worked out branding deals with everyone from Echo clothing line to an equity share in Vitamin Water for his "Formula 50" sports drink. (Vitamin Water was subsequently purchased by Coca-Cola, earning 50 a reported $400 million!)

Hip-hop entrepreneurs realized early on the importance of taking advantage of segmented revenue streams. With rap recording sales falling from 100 million units in 2002 to 59 million in 2008, live shows, ring tones, and cultivating corporate branding opportunities are more important than ever.

Aligning themselves with artists through branding provides companies with the opportunity to bring relevancy to their brand and open a line of communication to another generation of consumers. Companies tend to be aggressive about finding appropriate branding partners, and the responsibility of the artist's manager is to work to find the brands that best share the values of their artists. There always has to be a certain level of authenticity when putting together artists with brands.

INSIDER TIP: LICENSING AND MARKETING

The "Pink Moon" commercial is a great example of the synergy between licensing, marketing, and sales. Placements in TV, commercials, or film are something that practically any artist at any level can achieve as well, with a little help. One of the major reasons to sign with a publishing company is for their work in helping to "exploit" your copyright (meaning actively place your composition in income-generating opportunities, like a commercial or TV show). But publishing deals tend to be hard to come by for artists that are just getting started, so other options for licensing your music could come from hiring a dedicated licensing company (such as Fundamental Music or Ocean Park Music Group, both located in L.A.) to work your music on a fee-per-placement basis, or working with an online partner like www.pumpaudio.com or www.rumblefish.com to connect your music with music supervisors. Songwriters are paid a negotiated rate (called the synchronization fee) for all placements, which varies depending on (1) where the song is placed, (2) how often it is used, and (3) how much of the song is used. Rates can fluctuate from a payment of $5 for using a song for a simple podcast license to $50,000 or more for a nationwide ad campaign.

Branding not only provides an artist with an added revenue source; it can also do wonders for the artist's career. One of the best examples is Volkswagen's use of the signature Nick Drake song "Pink Moon." Although critically acclaimed, Nick's record sales had always been lackluster. At the time of the VW commercial in 2000, sales of Nick's last record, *Pink Moon*, were at about 80 units a week. Created by fans of Nick's music at the

large Boston-based ad agency Arnold, the ad was almost univer-
sally praised as being so great that it didn't cheapen the song
or Drake's memory in the slightest. Weeks after the commercial
began running, Nick's entire catalog sales skyrocketed, with *Pink
Moon* jumping up to more than 4,000 copies a week! The success
energized his label, and a Phase 2 marketing plan was initiated
at retail, press, and movie theaters more than twenty-five years
after the original release of the record!

HOW MERCHANDISING WORKS, WHO'S INVOLVED, AND WHERE THE MONEY COMES FROM

All artists, even those signed to major labels (perhaps especially those signed to major labels) need to optimize all possible
revenue streams and understand that although being a musician is at its core a creative endeavor, it is also a business with
income, expenses, employees, and vendors. With all businesses,
one has to spend money to make money. Potentially, one of the
most lucrative moneymaking areas for artists is merchandise.

There are lots of things that are not completely in your control
(traffic at your show, positive press, your van breaking down
between gigs), but band merchandise is something that you have
complete control over—unless, of course, you license your merch
rights to your label or a third party. What you sell and for how
much is up to you. In the live setting, you have a captive audience that you know is into what you do, and after you blow them
away with your completely amazing set, they'll be looking for
anything else they can get from you.

There are a few ways to go about selling your merch, mostly
dependent on where you are in your career, how much control
you want over the distribution of your image, the outlets where
your merch will be available, and the amount of resources you
have to successfully operate the merchandising arm of your
"company."

Merchandise on Your Own

Artists can handle all the merchandising themselves by working
directly with the printers and manufacturers. Many smaller
artists start off this way out of necessity, but some larger bands
like Phish, Guster, and Pearl Jam have also retained their
ability to create merch on their own behalf. Retaining the right
to create your own goods does a couple things. First, you're not
splitting the proceeds or getting a royalty on items you sell.
Second, artists that create their own merch have the freedom to
work with whomever they want, as well as have complete control
of quantities and distribution. But remember, with this added

freedom comes work, responsibility, and risk. Anyone who has ever created merch knows that things do not always come out as planned. It can be difficult to overcome when you receive a shipment of shrunken shirts two days before the start of your tour. Creating merch is a time-consuming process, and many artists opt to receive a royalty from merchandisers and focus on other areas of their music and business. Worst of all, artists can take a major financial hit if they overproduce items or create unpopular items that don't sell.

Working with a Merchandiser

Many larger or more established artists will work directly with a merchandiser themselves to license the right to use their image and create merchandise on their behalf. Merchandisers typically take a percentage of the total sales (usually around 30 percent) and provide an advance against projected earnings, which, similar to a record label advance, is recoupable from sales.

While any band that works with a merchandiser definitely loses some flexibility and control of how its image is distributed, there are several positive benefits to this agreement:

- The advance on future sales provides an influx of cash and is a great positive line item that artists can use to fund their tour.

- Merchandisers also can provide a better margin on goods because of the volume that they create.

- In addition to their Web presence, merchandisers have a broad network of global outlets that they are able to license your merch out to.

Having Your Label Handle Your Merchandise

Finally, it's not unusual for a record label to request exclusive merchandising rights when negotiating a contract with a band. All deals are different, but usually a label that negotiates merchandising rights from a band will then work as the licensee with a merchandiser to manufacture and sell merchandise displaying a band's image and trademarks in return for a fee. The fee is then split between the label and artist in a predetermined manner.

This type of arrangement is the least lucrative for a band for many reasons. Other than the fact that the label is taking a cut of the merch sales in their "middleman" role, in many cases royalties from merch sales are cross-collateralized with record royalties, meaning you're not going to see any dough from merch sales until your record is recouped. However, this is a pretty hard-core, old school way for labels to operate. Many of the larger indie labels are a bit more artist-friendly and leave these types of merch deals out of their record contracts.

BRANDON BUSH ON TOURING AND MERCHANDISING AS A REVENUE STREAM

Brandon Bush knows the importance of a solid merchandising plan. He's been a touring musician for over a decade; most recently as a member of the Grammy-winning band Train as well as the touring keyboardist for country music superstars Sugarland.

> *"Merchandise sales are such an interesting part of the music business. What you're aiming for is a figure per head at your show for your merch. My experience is that if you have the right demographic in your music and your merchandise is put together in the right way to serve that demographic, then it can become a very healthy and important part of your business. But if any of those elements don't line up, I think it becomes an expense to push the name of your brand. There is only so much room in your truck for t-shirts that you're not selling. In the 1980s, in hair metal bands, it was a no-brainer; your expensive rock t-shirt was a given. It's not true these days. With this economy, people are hurting. They've already spent all this money to come to the show, to park, to buy beer. It's hard to sell a $40 t-shirt. But if your fans believe in you as a band and you have good merchandise, then you're selling to people who love you, and you're selling them something that they're excited about. I think that's a healthy part of the business."*

PUTTING TOGETHER YOUR PLAN: WHAT TO MAKE, WHAT NOT TO MAKE, HOW MUCH TO MAKE, HOW TO MAKE IT

If you are an artist just starting out, you are going to be handling your merchandising yourself—solely responsible for all creative and financial decisions. If you've provided your merchandising rights to your label to license out, or licensed the rights out to a merchandiser yourself, your involvement in the merch process might be limited. You'll likely be only working with the label and merchandiser (sometimes to a limited degree) to find artwork and products that you feel comfortable with, and collecting your royalty on items sold. But if you are going your own way, from item idea to manufacturing to keeping to a budget, you are going to need to create a plan.

What to Make?

Essential	*Nonessential*
• recordings	• hoodies
• t-shirts	• guitar picks
• posters (signed and/ or limited edition)	• coffee mugs
	• hats
	• keychains
	• programs
	• magnets
	• anything that costs you more than $15 or $20 to create

First, the Essentials

Recorded music, t-shirts, and posters should always be the front line of your merchandising army. They offer the best opportunity to satiate your existing fan base's hunger for something from you, and provide the best advertising potential at relatively inexpensive prices.

Recordings. Recordings are a given. The first step is to have your complete discography (or if you are especially prolific, a selected discography) available at your gigs. Existing fans can fill in any holes in their collection (and feel good about themselves because they are buying direct from you), and folks that you have converted into fans can take your music home with them and turn on other folks. Definitely highlight your newest release, perhaps with sale pricing. It also makes sense to make some "tour only" releases. EPs (Extended Play, a release that typically contains only 3 to 5 songs) are a great opportunity to whet people's appetite when you're between proper full-length releases. If you add in some bonus cuts that don't make it onto your full-length album, these become collectable.

Remember, there is no shame in a homemade run of CDs to sell exclusively at your shows. Colin Meloy, the main songwriter in the Decemberists, was selling a tour-only, homemade CD of Morrissey covers! Now, who can possibly pass that up? The more personal, the better, cost willing. Vinyl can also be another good option. Close to a million vinyl records were sold in 2007, up almost 16 percent from 2006!

INSIDER TIP: SELLING CDs AT SHOWS

CDs sales at shows can also be submitted to SoundScan, an online service owned by Nielsen (best known as the company that rates the popularity of television programs), which tracks the sales of music and video releases. Label folks base a lot of their opinions on past band sales, and any SoundScan sales history can work in your favor if you eventually want to sign with a label.

T-Shirts. T-shirts are another no-brainer—a great source of income for you, as well as an excellent branding/advertising opportunity. There are a couple of things to consider when creating shirts. First, know your market. If your fans are older men, you may want to be heavier (pun intended) on the x-large shirts. If your fans are women or younger kids, customize to them. Indie kids tend to like their t-shirts tight fitting, so stay away from the XLs. Customization and creating cool looking stuff is key in all areas of merch. Also, black shirts tend to sell better than any other color of shirts (strange, but true!). T-shirts will typically run you from $3 to $5 each for basic, short sleeve, one-color, one-location logo, and up to $12 or more for long-sleeve ringer tees.

Posters. More advertising for you, and something cool for folks to hang in their dorm, office, etc. You can reuse posters that you have initially created to support your release at retail (more on this later), but also consider making limited-edition signed posters, or nicer numbered prints, if you are friends with a great artist. Down and dirty (no frills) posters can cost you around $0.80 each at a run of 1,000.

Nonessential Items

Once you've got a routine down and can pretty accurately predict sales on your essential items, it might make sense to insert some nonessential items into the mix. Hoodies are a popular choice, but their price point is quite a bit higher than t-shirts. Keep in mind, you are likely going to have limited space to sell your goods at a booth on tour, and carting around a lot of higher priced, larger items that you might not be able to display properly isn't a great idea.

What Not to Make

It's common for artists that are starting out to want to make creative and unusual items for their fans. And while the band's hearts may be in the right place from a financial standpoint, it's not the best idea to create unusual, high-priced tchotchkes. I've seen emerging artists that have tried to sell branded metal lunch boxes at live shows. It's a different story if you can draw a thousand folks to your gig, but if you are playing smaller club dates, it makes more sense to play it safe.

How Much to Make?

Determining the appropriate quantity is important. Until you have a handle on the average amount of promo items you'll sell, you really have to be cautious about what you make. Start off with relatively limited quantities. If you're playing 15 small dates over the summer, do you really need 5,000 copies of your CD on hand? Take a good look at your tour schedule over the next few months, and estimate what makes sense. If you are selling merch online off your Web site, or using merch as a street marketing incentive, factor those numbers in, too. And although manufacturing costs may be slightly higher at lower quantities, you'll win in the long run by having up-to-date materials. And keep in mind: ordering additional t-shirts and posters can be turned around pretty quickly if you notice that you are going through materials faster than you anticipated.

Here are some typical costs of common promo items from three different vendors, at various quantities:

Merchandise	Vendor 1	Vendor 2	Vendor 3
Generic T-shirts			
100 t-shirts	$7.65	$5.00	$4.70
			(all costs per unit)
200–499 t-shirts	$6.75	$4.50	$4.45
500 t-shirts	$5.85	$4.25	$4.20
Ringer T-shirts			
100 t-shirts	$9.55	$9.75	$7.20
200–499 t-shirts	$8.15	$9.50	$6.95
500 t-shirts	$7.45	$9.30	$6.70
Women's Ringer shirts w/cropped sleeves			
100 t-shirts	$8.80	$7.00	$6.45
200-499 t-shirts	$7.50	$6.70	$6.20
500 t-shirts	$6.80	$6.55	$5.95

Messenger Bags

100 bags	$18.95	N/A	N/A
250 bags	$17.95	N/A	N/A
500 bags	$17.15	N/A	N/A

Mesh Cap

100 caps	$7.50	$6.20	$3.75
250 caps	$6.65	$5.90	$3.50
500 caps	$6.15	$5.75	$3.25

Fatigue Cap

100 caps	N/A	$6.35	$6.00
250 caps	N/A	$6.10	$5.75
500 caps	N/A	$5.95	$5.50

Die-Cut Stickers

2500 stickers	$0.43	N/A	N/A
5000 stickers	$0.37	N/A	N/A

How to Make It?

In terms of professional commercial CDs and EPs, many labels use Cinram for CD duplication and Ivy Hill for the booklets for their audio titles, but the minimum run at these places may be a bit high to be cost-effective for an independent musician. In terms of CD duplication, a couple of outlets independent musicians might want to consider are www.superdups.com based in New Hampshire, and www.diskfaktory.com based in California. Both these outlets allow for a limited print run (as low as one-hundred copies) and are reasonably priced.

There are numerous merch manufacturing companies that deal with all sorts of companies, music and nonmusic alike, like Blue Wave (www.bluewavemarketing.com/) in Boston, and Jakprints (www.jakprints.com/) in Cleveland. Factory Merchandising (www.factorymerch.com) in California is a merchandise manufacturing company that is exclusive to the music industry. Factory Merch has worked with the Hives, Something Corporate, New Found Glory, and Jimmy Eat World. It has the advantage over other nonmusic focused vendors of understanding the intricacies of a proper merch supply line to artists on tour, and has worked out deals with shipping companies to keep costs to a minimum. They can also suggest popular items based on what has been successful for other artists.

MERCHANDISING SALES AND DISTRIBUTION STRATEGIES

Like any business, your band's "product" (in this case, merchandise) needs to have an effective sales and distribution strategy to have the greatest reach to your potential customers. A band should look at their merchandise as a dedicated revenue stream that deserves the same marketing and sales attention as anything else it does to make money. And just like selling a CD, all nonmusic-related merch needs the proper positioning, price, and promotion to be successful.

INSIDER TIP: THE REACH OF A MERCHANDISER

Again, if you are working with a merchandiser, you've already provided them with the right to exploit your merchandise with your likeness to their dedicated outlets. A merchandiser's reach is far and wide. In addition to working with larger venues across the world, merchandisers distribute products to major online and physical retailers/mall outlets such as Hot Topic and Spencer Gifts.

Selling Your Merch at Shows

Pricing

Unless you've priced and positioned your items properly, all the time you've spent researching, designing, and creating your merch is wasted. Because merchandise is an effective advertising vehicle as well as an income-generating opportunity, there are two distinct schools of thought when it comes to pricing merch.

A lot of artists choose to look at their merch as a way to spread the word about their band organically. As such, they price their items very aggressively (low—but enough to cover costs) to increase sales, but take a hit on the profitability of the item. The flip side of this is artists that bleed as much as they can from their merch sales, and then run the risk of alienating their fans and decreasing their sales.

Pricing your gear has a lot to do with where you are in your career and what kind of fans you attract. Sting, for example, really doesn't need to worry about advertising himself, and his fan base tends to be older folks that might have a bit of cash. For them, a $40 t-shirt isn't an incredibly big deal.

There are more variables involved for artists that are still building their communities. Emerging artists need the extra income that merch can provide to help fund their tour, but they also need to continue to build up their community through this added visibility so that there are more folks in the venue next time they play the market. While you might expect to see a $25 t-shirt at a Wilco show, if you priced the same shirt at a less notable band's concert, your sales would be in the tank. Smaller to mid-level artists should probably price their t-shirts somewhere around $12, which is relatively standard for artists that play smaller clubs up to 850 to 1,000 capacity. Keep in mind that most venues also charge a fee of 25 percent or so for the luxury of selling your nonmusic merch at their venue. Factor that into your bottom line as well.

Positioning

The merchandise table at venues is going to be small, and more than likely, you'll be sharing the space with other bands as well. Merch items that you want to sell (like your new CD, or limited edition EP/single) should always be front and center, perhaps with sale pricing. Take advantage of any signage or areas where you can highlight all your offerings. Also, it's easier to keep a spinning wheel, um, spinning, so if you find that one of your items is selling better than anything else you've made, make that item as prominent as possible.

Selling Your Merch Online

Music industry blogger Andrew Dubber recently said of MySpace, "MySpace is like a bar. It's a great place to talk and meet people, but if you want to get any real business done, you have to take your new friends home (your own site)." This is especially true of merch sales. Your own Web site should be optimized in a number of ways, and high up on the list is an area where folks can buy your merch.

There are a couple ways to go about this:

1. Set up your own online store using PayPal.

Pros

- You keep all the proceeds from your sales
- Easy to set up

Cons

- An amazing hassle if you are a small organization and are selling items online at a good clip

2. Work with an online fulfillment company.

Pros

- Someone who knows what they are doing is taking care of the back-end programming and e-commerce
- Simple to add new items to your store
- Easy ways to track inventory in most cases
- Customer service

Cons

- Fees/potentially high costs
- Uncertain shipping times
- Uncertain quality of merch in some instances
- Questionable licensing practices

Merchandisers all have their own flashy e-commerce sites, and in most cases, artists that work with a merchandiser can help to create a branded page on the merchandiser's site where their items can be sold. There are a number of options for the independent musician not working with merchandisers to accomplish the same thing. Some are better than others.

Basic Online Fulfillment/Merch Companies

Café Press and Zazzle are two of the most popular basic online fulfillment and print on demand manufacturing companies. They provide a super easy way to create an online store, upload your graphics onto selected items, and begin selling merch online for no money up front. Financially, they both operate in a similar manner: customers purchase their goods for a set price (currently, $16.99 for an organic cotton short sleeve t-shirt plus one imprint at Café Press, for example), and you are free to sell the item for whatever price you want in your online store that they set up for you.

While it can't get much easier to create an online store, neither Café Press nor Zazzle are set up for touring musicians. Online fulfillment should work in tandem with your tour, and one of the major benefits of online e-commerce is that you can unload unsold tour merch online (where instead of taking up warehouse space, it can now be marketed as collectable!). Café Press and Zazzle don't provide the ability to upload items that are not part of the standard items they sell.

Financially, it's not feasible to purchase a $16.99 shirt from Café Press to sell on your own, as the shirts are already marked up higher than what many fans would pay even without you taking any profit. Also, shipping costs are an astronomical $5 on a single shirt at Café Press. Lastly, in some cases, there are questionable licensing agreements associated with these basic companies. If you use Zazzle, you grant them a "nonexclusive, worldwide, transferable, **perpetual**, **irrevocable** license to copy, crop, reproduce, publicly display, sell, and distribute the Work and a **Changed Work** (if applicable) in various sizes and in any manner including, without limitation, via the Web site, **other Web sites**, and/or through multiple levels of distributors and through retail and wholesale channels, in, on, or as part of Products made by or for Zazzle (the 'License')."

It is never wise to sign a perpetual and irrevocable license to a merch company, especially one that can change your artwork (!) and sell your product wherever they want! Who knows, you might become huge and want the right to license your image to Hot Topic yourself!

Online Fulfillment Companies for Musicians

There do exist, of course, legitimate online merchandising and fulfillment companies that are reliable and understand the needs of the musician.

For $30 a month and a 14.5 percent cut of sales, Pro Merchandise, a division of In Ticketing, creates a custom Web page and online fulfillment system that artists can send 90 days' worth of inventory to, for online sales. While they are not a merchandising company, they provide full customer support for their online fulfillment system, and a trackable inventory system, so you can replenish your goods when you are running low. Another popular option is offered by Big Cartel, who charge $9.99 per month to host an online merch store (but requires that the artists send out the merchandise themselves).

One of the more artist-friendly, true merch/fulfillment options is through Factory Merchandising. Factory Merch works closely with an online fulfillment company called Merchsquad. Merchsquad creates your merch sales Web page; Factory Merch supplies Merchsquad with the gear, and Merchsquad reorders when products get low. In this arrangement, your manufacturing partner works directly with your fulfillment partner. They are speaking to one another on a regular basis, using the same language. Artists can group their tour merch and store merch orders together into a single print run to earn a higher volume discount, and artists can also send any leftover tour merch directly to their online store. Merchsquad charges 15 percent of the total sale to package, ship, and handle all payments. They also provide monthly sales reporting so you can see how your sales are going.

Summary

It's important for artists to recognize that in addition to creating music, they are also creating a brand. The partnerships they engage in and the merchandise they produce all tie back into this brand. Merchandising can be used as both a marketing and advertising vehicle, as well as a tool to fund other activities. There are several options available for musicians to create or license their merch, a number of merchandise distribution and pricing options, and many ways to fulfill your online sales.

In the next chapter, we'll look at one of the fastest growing areas in the new music economy: digital retail and distribution.

Workshop

- Research a popular band online. Are they handling their own merchandising? If not, can you tell who is? What interesting ways are they marketing their merch?

- Several established artists have not licensed their rights to merchandisers. Other than retaining more financial and creative control over their merch, for what other reasons might established artists retain this license? Can you identify any other nationally or internationally touring artists that are not working with a merchandiser?

- What items do you think would be most appropriate for you to produce and why?

- Does it make sense for you to work with a merchandiser?

- What is the most cost-effective item you could make that would best promote your band? Is there anything particular to your fan base that you should think about when creating your merch?

- What would be the most effective way for you to sell your merch, given your current situation?

3 How to Sell Your Music Online: Digital Retailers and Distributors

There's never been a more exciting (and uncertain!) time in the world of music distribution. While traditional CD sales continue to fall, worldwide digital sales have mushroomed to $2.9 billion in 2007, up from $20 million in 2003, according to IFPI, a U.K.-based record industry group. While not enough to offset the financial loss of physical sales, the doomsday predictions of the death of the music industry seem to be "exaggerated," as Mark Twain might say.

Online music retail is moving forward at a staggering pace. iTunes is currently the largest music store in the United States. And don't forget, iTunes launched in 2003. This was accomplished in less than six years!

Distributors act as the "middlemen" between the artist and the retail outlet. All retailers, both physical and online, require distributors to deliver the music to them; it would simply be too difficult from an operations as well as an accounting standpoint for retailers to work directly with artists. The Web has spawned thousands of artist-focused, online retail outlets, distribution mechanisms, and marketing avenues that all artists, from independent artists on a limited budget, to former major label hit makers, can take full advantage of. Let's talk about the details.

DIGITAL DISTRIBUTION BASICS

What Is Distribution?

It's a given that all artists want to have their music heard by as many fans as possible. But in order to sell your music to a broad range of interested fans worldwide, you will need distribution.

Music distribution has always played a fundamental part of the overall music industry. In some cases, innovative sales and distribution tactics have been responsible for the rise of entire genres of music. Sir Coxsone Dodd, a Jamaican music producer, revolutionized the distribution of ska in the late 1950s and early 1960s in the ghettos of Kingston with his portable sound system concept. Coxsone would load up a truck with a generator, turntables, and huge speakers, and set up street parties where his DJs (which included future Jamaican hit makers Lee Scratch Perry,

Prince Buster, U-Roy, and King Stitt) would spin test pressings of tracks that he had produced at his own studio, Studio One.

If the response was positive at the street parties (which sometimes had several thousand people in attendance), Coxsone would release a limited edition blank label of the single. If that sold well, the single was released commercially. Because people were already familiar with the song through the sound system at the street parties, Coxsone already had a fan base ready to purchase the single when it was released.

These days, music distribution is handled at more of a "macro" level. Independent artists and labels hire music distributors (or work with those that they own) to get their music into the multitude of retail stores worldwide, and in most cases, pay these distributors a fee for their service. For many years, distributors have worked specifically with physical outlets: chain and independent record stores, and "special market" types of outlets (alternative stores that happen to sell music—for example, a store that specializes in West African art might also want to sell CDs of Ali Farka Touré from Mali, West Africa). Currently, physical distribution at brick-and-mortar retailers is still the dominant way that most consumers buy their music. But the new kid on the block (digital distribution) is growing at an amazing pace, and in many ways, is leveling the playing field for independent musicians and labels.

With the rise of online music, music distribution is anything but traditional. There are more new players, formats, outlets, and partnerships than ever before, and similar to the weather in London, if you don't like what is happening now, wait a few minutes and it will all change.

Basic Digital Distribution Terms and Concepts You Need to Know

Just like traditional physical distribution, online distribution has its own language that is important to understand in order to utilize the services properly. Before we move into the intricacies of digital sales and distribution, let's get these foundational terms under our belt.

Compression

A commercially released CD has a lot of data on it—about 10 MB (megabytes) for every minute of stereo sound. A typical song could run 50 MB. This is a large file, and while debated by audiophiles, many experts feel that much of that data on a CD is not necessary. Compression makes the file smaller by removing some of the unnecessary aspects of sound that many consumers will not miss. In many cases, it reduces the file size down to a more reasonable 3 to 7 MB. Compression not only allows for a speedier delivery of music files over the Internet, but it allows for folks to store much more music on their computers and portable music players.

Common Uncompressed and Compressed File Formats

Uncompressed digital files are typically recognized as WAV or AIFF files. With compressed file formats, the amount your file is compressed directly affects the ability of your digital listening device to reproduce the music faithfully. The sampling rate of a digital music file is a way to describe how compressed your file is, and how precisely a file reproduces the analog sound it represents. Sampling rate is represented in groups of 1000 bytes that are captured from the music by your computer per second (kilobits per second), or "kbps."

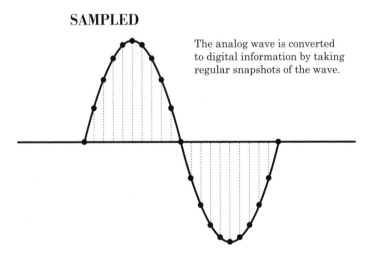

SAMPLED

The analog wave is converted to digital information by taking regular snapshots of the wave.

Fig. 3.1. Sampling

INSIDER TIP: SPACE CONSIDERATIONS FOR DIGITAL MUSIC PLAYERS

If you were a purist and only wanted to have uncompressed music in your digital music player, you would only be able to fit about two albums per GB (average of 50 MB per song, x 10 songs = 500 MB, and 1 GB = 1000 MB)! Not too many people would be happy with only 32 albums on their 16 GB iPhone!

Common Compressed Formats

MP3: Common format that can be played on all portable music players. Typical sampling rates are 128 kbps (average sound quality), 192 (better), and 256 (very good).

AAC: Apple's compression format. AAC was developed after the MP3 format, and is generally described as having a more efficient compression scheme with less audible quality loss than MP3s of the same file size.

WMA: Microsoft's compressed format. You have to use Microsoft Windows Media Player to encode WMA files, but many software players can then decode and play back your music.

FLAC: A "lossless" compressed file with no loss of sound quality. This is a big, but manageable file.

Apple Lossless: The highest-quality music format that Apple produces.

DRM

A major issue for years, DRM (Digital Rights Management), as it applies to music files, seems to be drawing its last breaths. DRM is a broad term used to describe any technology used to limit the use of software, music, movies, or other digital data. DRM interferes with interoperability between music purchased at digital retailers and the ability to play these files on different digital music players, as well as the number of devices consumers are allowed to play these digital music files on. For example, until January 2009, Apple's iTunes used a DRM technology called FairPlay to encrypt its AAC audio files, which meant that only the iPod could support these encrypted files. Anyone that had purchased music from the iTunes store could only play these files on their computer using iTunes, or their iPod. The result was a confusing mess for consumers.

DRM has existed in its present format since 1998, when Congress passed the Digital Millennium Copyright Act (DMCA), an extension to United States copyright law. Provisions in the DMCA make it a federal crime "to circumvent protection afforded by a technological protection measure," and provide statutory damages "in the sum of not less than $200 or more than $2,500 per act of circumvention," with repeat offenders having to pay "up to triple the amount that would otherwise be awarded, as the court considers just." The DMCA was introduced as an attempt to protect the rights of copyright holders in the emerging world of digital distribution, but is now considered by many to be outdated and repressive towards innovation and convenience for consumers.

DRM has been widely unpopular with consumers. At the end of 2007, the major labels announced they would sell DRM-free music on Amazon's new MP3 store, with Rhapsody and Napster following suit in mid 2008, offering music from all four major labels DRM-free. Some DRM schemes have outright killed individual CD sales for some artists. In 2005, Sony released a copy protection technology called XCP, which automatically installed itself into PCs and secretly monitored for any illegal CD copying or burning. Word spread quickly about Sony's plans, and consequently consumers refused to purchase any discs with the XCP protection. Sales of Neil Diamond's Rick Ruben–produced *12 Songs* on Sony stalled, as did sales of Sony CDs by Celine Dion, Trey Anastasio, and Ricky Martin.

Metadata

In addition to the music on your digital file, there is certain information that travels with your digital file to identify your song, and provides a way to keep track of how many copies of your track, or album, have sold. This information is known as *metadata.*

Metadata basically refers to any information that travels with your digital music that is not the music itself. One of the most important pieces of metadata is your ISRC code.

An *ISRC* (International Standard Recording Code) is a unique, twelve-character alphanumeric "digital fingerprint" that stays with an individual recorded track forever, regardless of any changes in ownership of the track. ISRCs are added to the recording during the mastering stage, or at the encoding stage by whichever digital aggregator/distributor (more on this soon) you are using to deliver your recorded content to the retailer.

ISRC codes are used to trace sales of single tracks through digital distribution outlets like iTunes, as well as help to trace the owner of a recording who is owed royalties when their recording is used by Internet and Satellite radio.

UPC

A *UPC* (Universal Product Code or Barcode) represents the entire digital product, as opposed to just an individual digital track. UPC codes are also found on the back of the sound recording's physical packaging, and are used by both brick-and-mortar retailers and online outlets to gather and track sales information for the entire product. SoundScan compiles UPC sales data from thousands of physical and digital retail outlets in the U.S. and Canada (as well as sales from artists on tour) to compile its weekly list of music sales. These reports are an important ingredient in the weekly Billboard charts, and also factor into many A&R departments' decisions to sign an artist.

You can apply for an ISRC code from the RIAA (the Recording Industry Association of America). Bar codes are a bit trickier. It is possible for you to register as a company and receive your own UPC prefix from the UCC (Uniform Code Council), but it is probably not cost-effective. An easier way for an independent artist to get a bar code is to work with a distributor that has already purchased a company code, and can provide (free or for a small fee) UPC bar codes to the albums they are distributing.

ONLINE MUSIC RETAIL MODELS

Online music retail is still operating a bit like the Wild West. There are several different options currently available for music consumers to purchase music online (which they then own outright, or in some cases, rent) on an a la carte or subscription basis. Many of these stores charge consumers a different rate for the services they provide, and in turn, these online stores pay the artists (you, or your distributor). Let's look at the current models as they exist today, and the ways artists get paid.

Permanent Downloads

A permanent download is music that has been purchased from a digital store for use on a computer, digital music player, or other device. There are two ways that a content provider (i.e., an artist) will be paid by a service that provides permanent downloads to their users.

- **Fixed Pay Rate.** You get paid a set amount for every download made of your content.

- **Subscription Pay Rate.** You get paid a variable amount per download (commonly known as a *pro rata share*) depending on (a) how many songs were downloaded, (b) how much money was made by the store in the same period of time, and (c) expenses deducted.

The Fixed Pay Rate is pretty straightforward: the store takes a cut of any sales (iTunes currently takes 30 percent, and pays out the rest).

The Subscription Pay Rate is a slightly convoluted way to account for digital sales. Here's an example of this payment process in action. Say a digital store using a subscription pay rate model sells 400,000 digital downloads over three months. Over those same three months, this store takes in $100,000 in revenue from its subscribers. Over this period of time, each download is worth $0.25. The store's expenses come to $0.05 a track. This would mean each download is worth $0.20, which would then be lowered again by whatever fee the store takes as its share from each download. (Expenses are over and above this fee.) If the store charges its artists a 40 percent fee, this means that you would receive 60 percent of $0.20 over this three-month time frame: $0.12 per download. The amount of revenue that the store takes in can fluctuate based on the amount of subscribers they have over a given period of time. What this means is that while a download might be worth $0.12 at one pay period, it could easily fluctuate up or down for subsequent pay periods based on the number of subscribers the store has gained or lost and the income they bring in.

Temporary Usage

Users that acquire a song for temporary usage have the right to listen to the song, but they do not own it. In most cases, users pay a monthly fee for access to this music, and once they decide to stop paying this monthly fee, their access to this music is gone.

Two popular temporary usage examples are:

Stream. Users who subscribe to a music service using a stream need to have their media player or computer connected to the Internet in order to listen to their music.

Tethered Download. Users who subscribe to a music service using a tethered download are able to listen to their music on their computer and in some cases on their portable devices (although this is sometimes at a premium price point), even when they are not connected to the Internet as the media file resides on their computer or device. These users only have to be connected to the Internet once a month for their service to confirm that they have paid their monthly fee and to renew their licenses. Once they decide to stop paying this fee, their access to this music "times out" and is gone.

Streams and tethered downloads cannot be burned to a CD, and are considered limited usages.

Stores providing temporary usage music pay artists one of two ways:

- **A flat, per-play royalty rate, usually around $0.01 to $0.02 per usage. Streams/tethered downloads that are shorter than thirty seconds or thirty-second sound samples are generally considered promotional, and you will receive no royalty for them. Also, some online stores let potential customers stream complete songs for free, for promotional use. You will not be paid for this either.**

- **A pro-rata calculation, very similar to the subscription pay rate.**

Ad-Supported

Although this has been discussed for years, the ad-supported model is still in its infancy. The ad-supported model allows users to listen to music for free on a Web site that delivers ads concurrent with the play event. The amount of money the artists get when someone listens to their songs is either a calculation based upon the amount of income derived from the sale of these ads for the royalty period, divided by the number of downloads or streams, less expenses and fees; or a guaranteed penny-rate per-play minimum. Some subscription-model ad-supported services pay artists either a pro-rata share of a per-subscription minimum, or a percentage of ad revenue that is divvied up on a pro-rata basis.

ONLINE MUSIC RETAIL OUTLETS

The amount of online music retailers increases almost daily. And just like physical retail there are "superstores" with a broad range of music, and smaller online niche specialized stores (my favorite being digital.othermusic.com, amazing under-the-radar music). We're definitely still in the early stages of online music sales and distribution, but anyone that has read Chris Anderson's "Long Tail" article from December 2004 will tell you that online retail has some distinct advantages over physical retail.

Over and above the fact that online retail has many fewer expenses associated with it than physical retail, online stores have the benefit of unlimited "shelf space." There are only so many places to hold CDs or records in a brick-and-mortar retailer, and independent artists as well as independent labels are always fighting for this limited space (and paying a premium for highlighted space). With online retail, there's a level playing field and enough space for everyone.

Let's take a look at some of the major players in the digital retail world, how they operate, and how they pay artists.

iTunes

Since its inception in 2003, Apple's iTunes has revolutionized the music industry. It's the most popular way for consumers to acquire music online legally, and as we mentioned earlier, it is currently the largest retailer of music, period. The iTunes music store has become a far-reaching entity, and currently operates seven distinct stores servicing music to many areas around the world, including iTunes U.S., iTunes Canada, iTunes U.K., iTunes E.U. (selling music to Austria, Belgium, Denmark, Finland, France, Germany, Greece, Italy, Ireland, Luxembourg, Netherlands, Norway, Portugal, Spain, Sweden, and Switzerland), iTunes Japan, iTunes Australia, and iTunes New Zealand.

iTunes sells all its music in the permanent download model, with variable pricing at $0.69 for older catalog titles, $0.99 for current songs, and $1.29 for hits (in the U.S.). Generally, iTunes sells a majority of albums with 10 tracks or more at a fixed price of $9.99. Albums with less than 10 tracks usually sell for $0.99 times the number of tracks.

Artist Payment Rate for Sales on iTunes

iTunes uses the fixed pay rate model for all independent labels and artists. iTunes provides artists with a 70 percent cut of all music sold (for example $0.70 per song sold at $0.99 in the U.S. or $7.00 per album with 11 or more songs sold in its entirety).

INSIDER TIP: DIGITAL MUSIC SALES AND EXCHANGE RATES

iTunes (and other retailers that have international penetration) pay in the local currency rates of the country where the sale occurred. So, if the dollar is weak, sales in other countries where the local currency is strong might produce more money for you than tracks sold in the U.S. (if you are based in the U.S.).

Amazon MP3

Frustrated by Apple's dominance in the marketplace and their initial refusal to offer variable pricing on their artists, the major labels backed Amazon in late 2007 with their Amazon MP3 store. With DRM-free higher quality music from all four major labels, the site provides a convenient alternative to iTunes.

Amazon MP3 uses the permanent download model to sell its individual songs and albums. It offers artists the ability to choose four different pricing levels (based on the pricing models that labels have used at traditional retail for years):

- Front Line: A-level new release pricing, most expensive
- Mid Line: B-level new release pricing, less expensive
- Catalog: Older release pricing, discounted
- Special: Promotional price, the lowest price in the store

Artist Payment Rate for Sales on Amazon

The payment rate for artists varies depending on the pricing level chosen. For example, artists that choose the "catalog" pricing level, which sells whole digital albums at $6.99 and singles at $0.89, receive 70 percent of the gross: $4.90 and $0.63 respectively per sale. Similar to iTunes, the model is based on the traditional physical record store percentage of sales: 30 percent. For independent artists, each album can only be sold at one level, and all songs on that album will be sold at that level. Amazon also does not offer regular or scheduled opportunities to change an album's pricing level.

eMusic

For many independent artists and labels, eMusic is the second largest income generator for digital music. Owned by Dimensional Associates (who also own the Orchard, which we will talk about shortly), eMusic was founded in 1998 as a DRM-free MP3 destination. Because of the lack of digital rights management, the major labels initially refused to work with eMusic. As a result, the store specializes in underground and nonmainstream offerings. According to eMusic, 74 percent of their users are more likely to download complete albums on eMusic than iTunes, and their subscribers spend, on average, $160 per year, compared to $7 per year spent by iTunes users. Ninety-one percent of eMusic subscribers say the low subscription cost encourages them to try music they have never heard before.

eMusic lets people download music on a pre-buy basis, which means that users pay a set fee up front for a certain amount of downloads. Currently, there are three options for users:

- eMusic Basic: 30 songs per month for $9.99 ($0.33 per song)
- eMusic Plus: 50 songs per month for $14.99 ($0.30 per song)
- eMusic Premium: 75 songs per month for $19.99 ($0.27 per song)

If a user does not use up his or her allotted songs per month, the leftover songs expire.

Artist Payment Rate for Sales on eMusic

Because songs are purchased at different rates by users depending on how extensive their subscription is, eMusic uses the subscription pay rate model to calculate what each track is worth over any given time period.

Napster

Napster was started by Northeastern University student Shawn Fanning in 1998. In the spring of 2000, the RIAA (backed by several big name artists, most notably, Metallica) took Napster to court over copyright infringement. After being shut down as a free service in 2001, Napster reinvented itself as a legitimate service for users to access digital music. Originally offering music encoded in Microsoft's PlaysForSure DRM-protected format, Napster began selling their tracks as DRM-free MP3s in 2008. Napster currently offers two models for its users: the streaming model, where users can listen to an unlimited amount of music while connected to the Internet, and the permanent download model, where users can purchase DRM-free permanent digital downloads (at $0.99 per track, in the U.S.). Napster pays on a monthly basis for permanent downloads, but pays on a three-month basis for streams.

Napster currently operates in the U.S., Canada, U.K., and Europe.

Artist Payment Rate for Sales on Napster

Napster pays artists in two ways:

- Every time a Napster user streams your music, you'll be paid a flat, per-stream royalty rate, usually around $0.01 to $0.02 per stream.

- Every time a Napster user permanently downloads your music, you'll receive Napster's Fixed Pay Rate. In the U.S., this rate is currently $0.65 per track, and $6.50 per album of 11 tracks or more.

INTERVIEW: BOB JAMIESON,
FORMER CEO OF RCA/BMG

Bob Jamieson, former CEO of RCA Music Group, BMG North America, is a respected leader in the music industry with over thirty years of experience both in the U.S. and abroad. He has helped launch and establish many well-known bands, including the Dave Matthews Band, Christina Aguilera, NSYNC, and Bon Jovi. He is currently on the board of several forward-thinking music business operations. Bob was running RCA when Napster was originally released in the late 1990s. The following is an excerpt from an interview with Bob about what went wrong with the first iteration of Napster.

You were leading RCA when Napster arrived on the scene in the late 1990s. It seems like the majors could have found a way to monetize and work with Napster instead of taking them out.

You know, Shawn Fanning actually started Napster to trade Dave Matthews live recordings; he is one of the biggest Dave Matthews fans in the world. Dave allows people to tape and trade the band's shows and Shawn wanted as many live recordings as possible, which is what prompted him and his programmer to develop Napster. Then the lawyers and everyone else got involved and the rest is history.

The reason that Napster had the problems they had was because of the "suits" involved with Shawn Fanning. The guys that took over the operations of the company at the beginning were really grinding the industry's face in the mud. Here they were, stealing the artist's music and acting like it was their right. They were so disrespectful that the industry had to slap them hard. Bertelsmann ended up owning Napster for a while and had a plan to launch an industry-run legitimate service like iTunes. The vision was good, but the execution was horrible. The idea was to create a universal file-sharing apparatus that the industry would co-own. Everybody would put their product through Napster— we would regulate it and monetize it in a way similar to iTunes or any of the other legit services. But instead, the industry was so mad at the original people involved with Napster, it never materialized. Looking back, if the industry had embraced the technology earlier and recognized what Napster was doing, we all would have been in better shape. It still would have changed the industry forever, and there still would have been a lot of suffering with people losing their jobs and careers, but it might have been done in a more logical and slightly less painful way.

Rhapsody

Rhapsody is Real Networks' online music service. Launched in 2001, Rhapsody offers users several different options for buying music online, and utilizes both the streaming and permanent download models. Rhapsody has partnered with a number of industry heavyweights including Verizon, MTV, iLike, and Yahoo.

Current options for Rhapsody users include:

Subscribers

- Rhapsody subscribers have the option of listening to an unlimited amount of music while they are connected to the Internet, and download an unlimited amount of music to their PC, which they can listen to online or offline, as long as their subscription is current. Subscribers are "renting" this music—it cannot be burned or saved in any way. Subscribers can also purchase permanent digital downloads.

Non-subscribers

- Non-subscribers can purchase songs on demand, but at a higher price than subscribers. Non-subscribers cannot stream songs on demand. Anyone that goes to Rhapsody's Web site can preview full tracks—up to twenty-five of them per month—before deciding whether or not to purchase.

Trial Subscribers

- Trial subscribers can try out Rhapsody's streaming service for fourteen days before they are asked to pay the subscription rate. Trial Subscribers can also purchase downloads at the same rate as subscribers: $0.99 per track.

Artist Payment Rate for Sales on Rhapsody

Rhapsody pays artists in two ways:

- When a Rhapsody user streams your music, you'll be paid a flat, per-stream royalty rate, usually around $0.01 to $0.02 per stream.

- Every time a Rhapsody user permanently downloads your music, you'll receive a payment, depending on what type of customer has downloaded your music.

- Rhapsody has a fourteen-day trial period where folks can get unlimited streams for free. This is considered promotional, and artists *are not paid* for any streams that users listen to while they are on this trial period.

Type of Rhapsody Customer | Income You Receive

- Subscriber Download: $0.65 per download

- Subscriber Stream: $0.01 per stream

- Non-Subscriber Download: $0.70 per download

- Trial Subscriber Download: $0.70 per download

- Trial Subscriber Stream: $0

ONLINE MUSIC DISTRIBUTORS

While some online retail models share similar traits to their physical counterparts (the pricing models of iTunes and Amazon mirror the pricing models of physical retail), there are fundamental differences between online and physical retail. One of the most important differences is that online retailers have unlimited shelf space, which provides an opportunity for anyone who has recorded an album to get his or her music onto one of these online services. However, if every artist that wanted to get their music up on these services tried to do it themselves, it would be an operational nightmare for the stores involved. This is one of the reasons that most all of the major online retailers will not accept music directly from an artist or smaller independent. These stores require that you work with a distributor who works as a middleman between the artist and the online store. It's easier for the store, and in the end, it's easier for you. Who can be bothered with keeping up to date with dozens of online stores and their different rules and procedures?

Online distributors come in many varieties. All the majors work with their own distribution companies that cover both online and brick-and-mortar retailers. Many of the larger indie labels work with these established major-owned independent distributors (like ADA, Caroline, RED, or Fontana) to accomplish the same thing. These deals are all negotiated between the artists, their label, and the distribution companies.

For independent artists and smaller independent labels, there are several options with relatively easy-to-understand terms and processes (which is so unlike the traditional record industry!). These online distributors can generally be categorized in two ways:

1. Online distributors that simply provide a vehicle to deliver your music and manage the relationship with the stores (sometimes called *DSPs* or *DMSs*, short for *digital service providers* or *digital music stores*), and collect your earnings.

2. Online distributors that provide a vehicle to deliver your music and manage the relationship with the stores, collect your earnings, and also provide a higher level of marketing or licensing support.

Let's look at some popular models for each of these categories of online distributors.

Basic Online Distributors

There are currently two established major players competing for a similar market of independent artists and labels for online distribution: CD Baby and TuneCore.

CD Baby

Founded by Berklee College of Music alumnus Derek Sivers, CD Baby has been in existence since 1998. The company began as a destination for independent artists to sell their physical CDs online (which it still does). CD Baby is the largest seller of independent CDs on the Web, and has paid over $87 million to artists for their physical and digital music sales.

Overview

As a digital distributor, CD Baby works with more than fifty online retailers. They take no rights from the content provider, they are nonexclusive, and artists can cancel anytime. There are also no annual charges associated with the service, and they do not have a per-delivery fee, which means that they will send your music to every retailer they work with without the price going up. They also have a staff of around one hundred, with over twenty people dedicated solely to artist services (fixing mismatched data, adjusting a wrong album cover that a retailer may use, etc.).

How It Works

Unlike some other digital distributors, CD Baby was designed to sell physical copies of CDs online. As a service to their members, they added digital distribution to the existing agreement they have with their members. Currently, there are two ways to get your music distributed to online retailers with CD Baby.

1. The traditional way for CD Baby to sell your music digitally is to add a digital option to your physical sales on the site. The process is very easy:

   - Fill out a submission form.
   - Pay a one-time fee of $35 per record you want to sell.
   - Mail CD Baby five CDs, one of which they digitize.
   - Sign up for the digital distribution option on CD Baby.
   - You will be set up with a CD Baby store and will also have your music digitized and delivered to all online sales outlets that CD Baby works with.

2. Have your music released digitally only.

   - Burn a finished mastered copy of your music onto a regular audio CD-R.
   - Sign it up at CD Baby as you would any other album.
   - Pay the setup cost.
   - Mail that one CD to CD Baby, with a note explaining that it is for digital distribution only.
   - E-mail the album cover/artwork.
   - CD Baby will add it to their system, like any other album, except it will be permanently out of stock on their site.
   - CD Baby digitizes the release and distributes it to all of the usual digital distribution outlets.

What CD Baby Charges for Its Service

CD Baby's charges are relatively transparent. The company charges a one-time fee of $35 for each album you want to sell (digital or physical). CD Baby also charges a 9 percent cut on any income generated through sales of your music using their service.

Other Fees

CD Baby charges $20 if you would like CD Baby to create a bar code for you.

How You Get Paid

Online stores generally pay monthly or quarterly. When CD Baby receives the sales report and payment on your music sold, it adds this amount to your account (less the 9 percent fee), and you are paid the week after CD Baby is.

HERE'S THE MATH: CD BABY

Say CD Baby distributes your music to iTunes, which sells 1,000 individual tracks of your music. If iTunes charges $0.99 per track, this would be $990 in total revenue generated. iTunes takes the cut first, which in the U.S. is $0.29 per track, leaving about $700 that is paid to CD Baby. CD Baby takes their 9 percent fee from this $700, leaving you with $637.

Yes, it's nonexclusive, but...

Both CD Baby and TuneCore offer nonexclusive deals to their members, which means that neither company will prevent you from using another distributor at any time. However, you cannot have more than one distributor bringing the same album to the same store. Otherwise, when the album sells, how would the store know which distributor to pay?

INTERVIEW: DEREK SIVERS, FOUNDER OF CD BABY

Derek Sivers founded CD Baby as a way to sell his own music off his Web site. Originally operated out of Derek's apartment in Woodstock, NY, CD Baby has grown to employ around one hundred people in the company's Portland, Oregon warehouse complex. In mid 2008, Derek sold CD Baby to CD-manufacturer Disc Makers.

How important is niche marketing for developing artists?

You can't cut through if you're well rounded. To cut through the world's apathy, you have to be sharply defined. Be so simple that someone could draw a recognizable cartoon character of you. If the thought of this rubs you the wrong way, consider making each album a sharply defined niche with a purpose. A bunch of niche/purpose/project albums over the years equals a very well rounded career, but each album will be much easier to market than if you're trying to be all things to everyone.

You founded CD Baby in 1998. How has the music industry changed since then?

Distribution is no longer an issue! That's a huge change! Only ten years ago, if you had an album's worth of songs, there was not a single company anywhere online that would let you sell it. Amazon only sold books. The online record stores only listed the catalog of the major labels and distributors. The only way to get your music available to anyone not in front of you was to sell your soul to a major distributor, if some executives found you worthy of their channels.

Now, it's the opposite: anyone anywhere can fart into a mic and upload it to hundreds of outlets for sale or download. So now, word of mouth has become the real distribution.

Do you see any downsides to this change?

There are no downsides at all. The music business has always been survival of the fittest. But before, survival of the fittest meant being the one who was able to schmooze and impress the corporate executives so they would allow you through their golden gates just to let people hear your music. Now, survival of the fittest means winning over music fans yourself—making something that fans love enough that they tell all their friends and open their wallets to buy. If you pass that test, then the corporate executives will pass you through to the next level.

What marketing techniques should artists particularly focus on to sell digital music?

When we first started getting sales reports back from iTunes, I was amazed to find that the top sellers on iTunes were not the top sellers on CDBaby.com. In fact, I didn't even recognize them! Some albums were selling $10,000 in downloads, but only $20 in CDs. It took a long time to realize the one thing these digital top sellers had in common: cover songs. All of them had done a cover version of a well-known song. Then it made sense. In a record store (like CDBaby.com), you browse by artist, by genre, by looking at album art, etc. But in iTunes, people type in the name of their favorite song into the search engine. If they typed "Wonderwall" because they love that Oasis song, and you've done a cover of Wonderwall, as previously unknown Melissa Rebronja did, now everyone searching for it only sees two versions: the one they know and the one they don't. Many are curious enough to check out your cover version, and voila! New fan! Many of these fans end up buying the whole album, so your cover song was just a beacon calling attention to your album.

I highly recommend every new artist do at least one cover song on each album from now on. Do iTunes research first, to make sure it's a song that hasn't been covered too much, then make sure your cover version sounds uniquely you, not like the original.

What similar traits do successful artists share?

Taking full responsibility for their own success. Meaning: there is no fairy godmother that will wave her magic wand and make you a star. Successful artists know that whether they are signed to a label or not, every single fan is won over one at a time by their own actions. Nobody else will make you successful. The only way you'll get successful is if you make yourself successful.

There are a number of different online retail models: sites that pay artists per permanent download, sites that pay per stream, subscription sites, and other variable payment rate sites. Is there any reason that artists should choose one online retail option over another? Does it make sense for artists to work with online retailers that are paying one or two cents per stream?

Absolutely! Remember this: there are millions of people who get all of their music from Rhapsody. If they search for you on Rhapsody, and you're not there, they'll forget you and move on. Same with eMusic. Same with iTunes. Same with Amazon, etc. So make sure you're available on all of these services. You are not hurting your iTunes sales by being on Rhapsody; you are only adding to your income.

Don't forget that streaming income is per play. So if someone transfers your song to their mobile device, then listens to it ten times while on the beach, next time they get online, it reports all ten plays, and you get paid ten times for those ten plays.

Should artists forgo a physical CD and focus exclusively on digital sales and distribution?

The real question is: How much of your potential audience are you willing to exclude?

We're in transitional times. A lot of people have iPods. But most still don't. A lot of people get all their music online. But most still don't. If you decide not to put your music on iTunes or Rhapsody (say, if you have cover songs and don't want to bother with the paperwork), your music will never be heard by the millions that get all their music on iTunes or Rhapsody.

But if you decide not to have your music on CD, your music will never be heard by the millions that still do all their listening on CD. (Even if they listen to streaming clips while sitting at their computer, they do all their real listening in the car, or on the home stereo.)

So, my current answer is: if you're serious about being a professional musician, you need to do both. If you're just playing around, and never expect even a hundred people to want your music, then just upload to MySpace like everyone else does, and don't make a CD.

But in these long-tail days with over five million artists on MySpace, having a professional CD—a beautifully designed and manufactured CD—really sets you apart and shows you're serious to anyone in the music industry receiving your CD. Investing $1,000 into manufacturing CDs shows that you plan to make at least $1,000 selling them. Not spending the $1,000 is like saying, "I don't think I'll ever make $1,000 doing this." Then you wonder why a booking agent or label is not interested?

To close with a telling example:

When visiting Apple iTunes, I had lunch with the guy who's in charge of independent music editorial—the one who chooses who gets featured placement.

I asked him, "What's the best way for me to turn you on to something I think you'll love?"

His answer? "Send me the CD."

I said, "Uh...really? What if it's already on iTunes? Shouldn't I just send you the link?"

He said, "Yeah. I commute an hour each way to Apple's office. I do all my real listening in the car, so I need the CD."

Do you think it is important for an artist to be a "jack-of-all-trades," to have Web skills, a publishing background, a legal background, a marketing background, etc., or does it make sense to put a team together that can handle some of these areas?

You have to do everything just barely enough to find and recognize someone who's better than you. Whatever you love doing, absolutely do it. But whatever drains you, find someone else to do it immediately. Maybe you love updating the Web site yourself. Then do it! Maybe you love booking the shows. Great! But get used to meeting a few new people every week who are great at what they do, especially for the things you don't love, so you can hand it to them.

What revenue streams do you feel are important for artists to focus on?

Any you can get! Really. Last time I had a job was 1992. I quit and committed to being a full-time musician. The only way to do it is to say "yes" to every single opportunity. Producing records, playing on other people's records, touring as a backup band, writing jingles, playing children's music, teaching lessons, whatever it takes!

CD Baby was an incredible entrepreneurial venture for you. What have you learned from the experience? What entrepreneurial advice can you give to artists that are trying to make it in the music business?

You'll know when you're onto something, because people will freak out over it. They will love it so much they'll tell everyone. If nobody's freaking out about it yet, don't waste time marketing it. Instead, keep improving until they are.

How do you see people listening and purchasing music in the future? What do you think will be the dominant music delivery platform?

The football has been fumbled, and all the players are diving in to the mud, trying to grab it. Nobody knows how things will look in five years or even next year! I don't know the future, and neither does anyone else.

TuneCore

TuneCore was founded in 2005 by Jeff Price, who also founded spinART records in the early 1990s (Frank Black, the Pixies, Apollo Sunshine, John Doe, the Apples in Stereo, Vic Chesnutt). He was formerly a director at eMusic, and helped to create and implement their subscription-based music sales structure.

Overview

TuneCore is a digital distributor that currently works with many popular online retail outlets, including iTunes, AmazonMP3, eMusic, Rhapsody, Amie Street, Lala, and the ring-tone provider GroupieTunes. Similar to CD Baby, TuneCore is nonexclusive, and takes no rights from the content provider. Secondary to its online distribution, TuneCore also provides manufacturing, promotional materials, and other partnerships to provide the artist with basic marketing support.

How It Works

- Upload your music and artwork on the TuneCore Web site.
- Choose where you would like your music distributed.

What TuneCore Charges for Its Service

TuneCore is set up differently than CD Baby. First, TuneCore does not take a percentage of any income from the sales of your digital music. Instead, TuneCore charges the following:

- $19.98 per album, per year
- $0.99 per song, per store, per region (iTunes has seven regions, for example)
- TuneCore also allows artists to deliver a single to all of their different digital music stores for a flat annual fee of $9.99.

Other Fees

TuneCore charges $20 as an early termination fee if you cancel your service within six months.

How You Get Paid

When TuneCore receives the sales report and payment on your music sold, they add this amount to your account. You can withdraw your balance and get paid whenever you want through PayPal.

HERE'S THE MATH: TUNECORE

Say TuneCore distributes your music to iTunes, which sells 1,000 individual tracks of your music. If iTunes charges $0.99 per track, this would be $990 in total revenue generated. iTunes takes the cut first, which in the U.S. is $0.29 per track, leaving about $700 that is paid to TuneCore. TuneCore pays this amount to you without taking any percentage.

Larger Online Distributors with Support Services

There is the notion among some in the industry that the core issue related to distribution comes down to the leverage your distributor has. There are several distribution options available for independent labels (less likely for individual artists unless they are smoking hot, or have a massive fan base). These "full service" distributors claim to work with their labels to support their releases through external marketing-related buzz, free promo deals, online support marketing, as well as have a more direct relationship with decision makers at the online stores to get better placement on the stores' Web sites.

The largest players in this market currently are IODA (Independent Online Distribution Alliance), the Orchard, IRIS, and INgrooves. Whereas CD Baby charges a flat 9 percent as a distribution fee, these full-service distributors charge quite a bit more, somewhere around the 15 percent (IODA), to 30 percent (the Orchard). Contracts are negotiated on a per-label basis.

IODA has a small marketing staff, which focuses on retail marketing (efforts to get featured placement on digital music sites) and digital marketing (blog and podcast promotion, Internet radio servicing). IODA has also created a site called Promonet, which is an area where bloggers, retailers, Internet radio programmers, podcasters, and other "tastemakers" can find promotional MP3s, which you provide free of charge, that these folks can use to promote your music.

Labels that IODA currently distributes include Absolutely Kosher (a great small label that released some amazing records by one of my favorite bands, Pinback), Ropeadope (Antibalas, Charlie Hunter, DJ Logic), and Six Degrees (fantastic world-music focused label).

The Orchard has a much larger marketing staff, even more so now with the purchase of their competitor Digital Music Group in late 2007. In addition to positioning themselves as a larger independent distributor with more leverage, The Orchard claims that its higher distribution percentage is validated by the fact that its licensing, promotions, and marketing attention will provide artists with more visibility and more revenue than if they tackled these promo outlets themselves.

The Orchard distributes labels including Dim Mak (Bloc Party), Barsuk (Menomena, Rocky Votolato), and Frenchkiss (Les Savy Fav).

INSIDER TIP: MARKETING MULTIPLE PROJECTS

Keep in mind that many services in the music industry, from full-service distributors to publicists to radio promo indies, promise a degree of visibility through their industry contacts. And while their contacts may be valid, it's also important to remember that these folks only have so many resources available to them. The Orchard distributes more than 80,000 titles. If you are a small label that is not making a lot of marketing noise already, the chances are high that they are going to focus their energies on servicing their larger clients.

Summary

There are broad and ever-changing digital sales and distribution options available to small labels and independent artists. It's important for artists to realize that there are significant differences in the payment models between retailers, and to choose their outlets carefully based on what they are looking for from their release: revenue, exposure, or both. Although still in its infancy, online distribution has proven to be one of the most effective Web-driven independent artists' tools to arise over the past ten years.

Workshop

TuneCore vs. CD Baby

- If you are currently in a band, what service do you think would be best for you and why? If you are not currently involved in a band, what service would you recommend to someone that is, and why?

- Using a round number of 1,000 tracks sold at $0.70 cents over the course of one month, is TuneCore or CD Baby a better choice for a band, financially speaking? Which is a better choice after one year? How does your opinion change if you were to sell 10,000 tracks in one month? Does your opinion change if you want more visibility internationally? Which distributor is an overall better choice for promotional opportunities? What are the other positives and negatives you see with these two distributors?

Larger Online Distributors with Benefits

- Do you feel the promotional benefits offered by full-service distributors justify the fee that these services charge?

- What kind of label or band do you feel would benefit from a full service distributor?

4 Traditional Brick-and-Mortar Distributors

As we learned in the last chapter, there is huge growth happening in online music distribution. There are new online retail outlets, new sales models, and new distributors popping up all the time. The cost of entry is low, and because there is unlimited shelf space, it's no problem for distributors to get your "product" onto the digital shelves of even the most popular online retailer.

Physical distribution (getting your CDs on the shelves of retailers nationally or internationally) is another story. More and more local and chain retailers are going out of business every year, and there are very few new retailers opening up to take their place. With this decrease in outlets, complicated by the fact that there are more than 700 releases a week that are fighting for limited shelf space, you can begin to see the difficulties that are inherent to physical distribution.

That being said, physical distribution is still a major part of a successful artist's marketing plan, once that artist has reached a certain degree of popularity and following in his or her music career. It is also a necessity for any band signed to an effective label; distribution and marketing are the key roles of a label. Though digital distribution is growing by leaps and bounds, there is an important point to remember: Physical sales of music still exceed digital sales, at this point.

PHYSICAL MUSIC DISTRIBUTORS: THE PROCESS AND THE PLAYERS

The Process

The role of the music distributor is pretty straightforward. Basically, the distributor works with a label (or an artist directly) to present and sell a music release to brick-and-mortar (as well as online) retailers. The distributor presents the merits of the artist to the retailer, takes orders from the individual stores, warehouses the product, ships the product, invoices the stores, prepares statements to the labels it distributes, and pays the label for sales. The distributor acts as a wholesaler between the labels/artists and the stores. In addition, a label could also send its distributor the master and artwork for a particular release and have the distributor manufacture the product for them. This type of distribution deal is called a P&D (pressing and distribution) deal.

The Players

There are three major categories of music distributors:

- major distributors
- independent distributors owned by majors
- true independent distributors

Major Distributors

The four major labels all have their own distribution companies:

EMI (Capitol, EMI) currently distributes labels including Capitol, EMI, Blue Note, and DCC. **Sony Music Entertainment/BMG** currently distributes labels including Sony, CBS, Epic, Columbia, Arista, RCA, and Zomba. **Universal** currently distributes labels including Geffen, ABKCO (which has the Rolling Stones classic releases), Island/Def Jam, Interscope, Verve, Narada, Universal, and MCA. **WEA** (Warner Bros., Elektra, and Atlantic) currently distributes labels including Warner, Atlantic, Elektra, Reprise, and Rhino.

Independent Distributors (that are owned by the majors)

An independent distributor owned by a major? It sounds a bit strange, but it makes sense. The idea is like this: Major label distribution outlets need to focus their energies on the Justin Timberlakes and 50 Cents of the world. They own "independent" distributors whose job it is to find profitable labels and artists that are under the major-label radar.

These independent distributors would say that the backing of a major label provides smaller labels with increased security (there is little chance that they will go bankrupt, unlike smaller, true independent distributors), which is true, but major label-owned independent distributors run the risk of also being more entrenched in the "We don't do that around here" old-school way of thinking.

Major label-owned independent distributors:

- ADA (Alternative Distribution Alliance): owned by Warner
- RED (Relativity Entertainment Distribution): owned by Sony
- Caroline: owned by EMI
- Fontana: owned by Universal

True Independent Distributors

Music distribution has not been immune to the changes that have occurred in the industry over the past few years. The larger independent distribution companies have slowly been disappearing. Ryko Distribution was purchased by Warner in 2006, and Navarre was purchased by Koch (now known as E1 Entertainment) in 2007, making E1 Distribution (as well as Redeye Distribution) one of the only "true" independent distributors with the kind of scale to compete with a major-owned independent.

There are thousands of smaller distributors and one-stops (which act as an intermediary between distributors and retailers). The smaller distributors and one-stops tend to be niche-based, focusing on "mom & pop" independent retail outlets.

Examples of smaller independent distributors include:

- Very: hardcore, metalcore, emo, punk

- Revolver: dance, indie

- Nail: Pacific northwest-based alternative, independent music

Distribution Organization

A moderate-sized distributor (E1 Distribution, ADA, Ryko Distribution) would have the following basic staff in place:

President: oversees the entire operation, acquires new labels/artists to distribute, sheds underperforming labels, sets the distribution fee

Regional Directors of Sales: oversee individual sales reps per region; handle larger chain or large regional independent chain accounts

Director of Marketing/Marketing Staff: works on positioning new releases with the retailers through several outlets, and communicates co-op (more on this concept soon) opportunities and requests to the labels and stores

Inventory Manager: communicates order requests to the manufacturer, ensures having the proper inventory on hand to supply the demand for a particular record

Regional Sales Reps: provide one-on-one personalized support to retail accounts in major markets, including Southwest, D.C., N.Y., Boston, L.A., S.F., Northeast, Chicago, Midwest, etc.

Phone Sales: maintain connections with buyers and store managers with updates and promo materials

WHEN DO YOU NEED PHYSICAL DISTRIBUTION?

Physical distribution follows marketing. It's all too common for an artist or label to think that once their CD is in the stores, the sales will start rolling in. This is the farthest thing from the truth, especially in this day and age with more releases than ever, and fewer retailers around. When Tower Records closed its doors a few years ago, it was a major blow to all the distributors, as there was one less major retail player to work with. Borders and Wal-Mart are also decreasing the shelf space allotted to music releases. Distributors are looking for surefire sellers, and competition is fierce.

On a national level, before a distributor will even consider working with a label, that label has to prove that it has the leverage, marketing support, and resources to move the releases from the shelves. For a new release, the distributor wants to know about key press support, radio plans, tour plans, special guests on the record, and what kind of sales background the artist has. The label has to create a demand for the release prior to distributors soliciting it to retailers for them to take it in, and continue the marketing heat throughout the life cycle of the release. Otherwise, the release will sit on the shelves unsold, and eventually be shipped back to the label as a return, making everyone unhappy. (More on this wonderfully vexing part of the industry soon....)

Additionally, marketing dollars alone won't move product off the shelves. There has to be a legitimate buzz in order for real sales to happen. It seems like a fundamental concept, but even the most established labels sometimes get this wrong. Although less common now, back in the age of record label excess, it was not unheard of for a label to blow upwards of a million dollars or more on a marketing campaign for an artist, pay for positioning at retail, and end up sitting on a pile of returns because there was no legitimate "need" for consumers to buy the CD. This is one of the casualties of a "shotgun" approach (as opposed to a niche-focused approach) to marketing that was common to major labels in the late 1990s: creating expensive videos for MTV, buying vans wrapped in the artists' name and image and driving it along South Beach in Miami during college spring break, or using top name producers to work on a record by a completely unknown artist. Without an organic fan base that is being targeted directly, the risk of a million dollar campaign that hinges on the success of a video or other nonpersonal marketing is very high.

INDEPENDENT ARTISTS AND DISTRIBUTION

It's very difficult for an independent artist to get national distribution through a major-supported or true independent distributor. In most cases, an independent artist does not have the money, leverage, or marketing knowledge in place to direct the distributor. Also, in order not to get burned, many larger national distributors require $1 million in annual revenue before they will consider you. More often than not, an independent artist will work with a smaller distributor on a consignment basis, where the artist will send the distributor several copies of his or her CD, and not be paid until these CDs sell (or are returned).

When things start to become unmanageable (in a good way)—when you can't press enough CDs to keep up with the demand you are creating from your own marketing efforts—then you know it is time to solicit the help of a larger distributor.

INSIDER TIP: UMBRELLA DISTRIBUTION GROUPS

So, you're in a white-hot band but are having trouble working out a distribution deal because you are not yet on the radar of a national distributor. Many artists in this position try to work with *umbrella groups*, which essentially are sub-distributors that work with a number of up-and-coming artists. Collectively, these umbrella groups are worthwhile to the distributor because they net upwards of $1 million annually, and are a great option for a popular independent band that wants nationally visibility. Dan Zanes is an example of a popular artist who works with an umbrella group (Virtual Label).

Independent artists that do work with the national distributors tend to have a lot going on, on their own. O.A.R., a jam band out of Ohio, had a *major* following with college students, and would routinely sell out 1,500-seat venues around the country. For a distributor, it's easy to walk into a retailer, point out the band's tour schedule, and have the retailer buy in. The band created its own leverage through an extremely heavy tour schedule and popular live shows.

 SPOTLIGHT: ERIC LEVIN
(CRIMINAL RECORDS)

Eric Levin, who runs Criminal Records in Atlanta, as well as a successful independent music network called AIMS, describes the role of retail in the initial success of NYC-based Clap Your Hands Say Yeah, broken by Pitchforkmedia.com, the online indie-rock based music review site.

Clap Your Hands Say Yeah is a good example of everything coming together: good press, good buzz, good touring—it's all part of it. Their manager happened to be a publicist, but the band's success was really driven by Pitchfork. The independent retailers went directly to the band and told them we wanted to sell their record, and we got the band wider distribution through our store's national network. Through that success, they got ADA distribution, and the band was broken; they were on their way.

THE DETAILS

Unlike the relative transparency of digital distribution, physical distribution has a number of convoluted practices, mostly related to returns of physical product from the retailer back to the distributor. Here are some of the details related to a common distribution deal with a larger distributor.

Pricing

Labels set the suggested retail list price (SRLP) for all their releases (which is what the artists royalty is based off, incidentally). If the artist is a developing artist, the SRLP will usually be lower than a more established artist. Distributors typically sell records for 30 percent less than the SRLP to the retailers, which is the wholesale price that distributors pay the label on.

Distribution Fee and How It Is Calculated

Similar to some online distributors, physical distributors charge a fee to get your music into the stores. And unlike online distributors, there is usually a fair amount of work that your distributor is doing on your behalf to earn this fee. The distribution fee that an independent distributor charges varies from label to label, usually from 14 percent (bottom-of-the-barrel fee that major label distributors charge their own labels) to somewhere closer to 30 percent.

Distribution fees are driven by volume and leverage: the more product by names that retailers are familiar with, the lower the fee. Distributors justify a higher distribution fee for lesser known labels and artists by the fact that they have a lot more work to do to sell an unknown release by someone with no track record. The more work a distributor has to do, generally speaking, the higher its distribution fee will be. It's not a ton of work for distributors to sell in the new Jay-Z record. The marketing has already been done: he's everywhere. Lesser known artists require a substantial amount of work. The distribution team has to introduce the artist to the retailers, present the artists' accomplishments intelligently, and follow up frequently on tour, press, and radio updates.

Returns Reserves

The concept of "returns" can make the entire retail industry seem like a racket. Unlike pretty much any other industry, the record industry allows retailers to return any unsold records back to the distributor at full price. Because of this, distributors hold a reserve against payables to the label on any sales they make. The reserve percentage varies depending on how well the distributor thinks a label will do in the long term, but for new labels, it is typical for a distributor to withhold 25 to 35 percent of gross sales for 90 days as a reserve against returns. Also, if a label happens to have an especially bad month where returns exceed sales, the label will not be paid until all returns have been washed out by sales. Retailers generally hold onto product for 90 days after street date before returning it.

Discounts

Distributors also have the right to discount a label's releases during specified "Sell In" Programs they have with retailers. Typical discounts are usually in the 6 to 10 percent range.

Manufacturing

If you enter into a P&D deal with your distributor, you will have this manufacturing cost deducted from your net payment as well. At higher runs, count on about $0.80 per unit.

Payment

The distributor pays the label on the wholesale price, less the returns reserve, less manufacturing (if you are in a P&D deal), and less any marketing or administrative costs, usually sixty to ninety days after the sales have taken place.

HERE'S THE MATH

Say your distributor sells 3,000 records in the month of July at a $10 wholesale price. The label's gross sales will be $30,000 (3,000 x $10). If the distributor is holding return reserves at 30 percent, the payable is now down to $21,000 (remember, these reserves will be liquidated three months down the line). If you factor in a manufacturing cost ($0.80 per unit) of $2,400 and a marketing/admin cost of $1,500, you are already down to $17,100 payable to you in September or October for sales that happened in July!

CO-OP

What Is Co-Op?

In principle, co-op is a shared (cooperate) expense that the distributor and retailer pay to promote a record in the stores. For example, a distributor would contribute $100 towards the cost of a $200 ad, and the retailer would kick in the remaining $100. However, in practice, co-op is not a shared expense at all. (I don't think it ever really was!) The distributor pays 100 percent of all expenses related to positioning and visibility for a release at retail; the retailer just needs to follow through on placing the visibility in the store, or in the third party outlets. Essentially, the distributor is subsidizing the retailer's ability to help promote an artist. But remember, the distributor always charges back the label for all co-op costs associated with any particular release.

INSIDER TIP: THE COST OF CO-OP

In order to get the proper visibility, many independent labels spend upwards of $2 per unit on a new artist's national retail campaign!

Co-Op Opportunities at Retail Include:

Listening Post. Occasionally, an independent retailer will have an "employee picks" listening post where the staff truly chooses the content in the post, but nine out of ten times, the releases in a listening post were placed there for a period of time through co-op money from the distributor.

Depending on the retail outlet, listening posts cost about $100 a month.

End Caps/Pricing/Positioning. An *end cap* is the highly visible area at the end of a row of CDs. Often, the releases that are in the end caps are also tagged in ads from the store. For example, the large Boston-based independent retail chain Newbury Comics has a "Sounds from the Underground" program that includes tags in print ads, as well as visibility on an end cap. Additionally, distributors offer special pricing incentives to retailers, where a CD would be on sale for a specified period of time. Of course the retailer is not shaving this sale price from its margin; the retailer is making up the difference in co-op dollars.

Co-Op Print Ads. As mentioned above, retailers place ads in local music-themed weeklies tagging new releases or catalog sales. These ads are paid for through co-op from the distributor. Best Buy, currently the third largest music retailer in the U.S., also has a circular that goes into eighty million newspapers nationally.

E-mail. Music fans find out about music in a number of ways, one of which is through e-mails directly from their favorite independent retailers. If you want to stay up to date with what the kids are listening to these days, I suggest signing up for Criminal Record's (Atlanta), Other Music's (NYC), and Luna's (Indiana) e-mail blasts. In addition to reviews of new releases by the store's staff (which is not paid for), there are paid banner ads placed by the distributors that are supported by co-op.

INSIDER TIP: FREE GOODS

Some distributors also pay for co-op visibility through Free Goods, which are essentially just what they sound like: CDs that the retailer receives for free in exchange for some marketing support. This practice is frowned upon by many distributors, as some stores never actually display the free goods (especially if they are from an up-and-coming band that no one has heard of before). It is not unheard of for a retailer to return these free goods for something that they are more likely to sell.

Now that you know about the potential co-op opportunities at retail, you would think it would be easy to pick a program that works, and give it a shot, right? Well, it's not that easy. There is fierce competition over these co-op spots. Distributors have to pitch a release to a retailer and wait for it to be approved before they can give the label's money to the store. Retailers make all the choices on positioning and visibility, and this visibility is usually dependent on pre-promotion by the label. This is the reason that labels start soliciting distributors four months out from the release with white-label burned advances and "industry only" showcases. Labels have to create an interest and demand from the distributors, who communicate this urgency to the retailers.

Creating Marketing Tools for Your Distributor

Catalog Advertisement and Distribution One-Sheet

Distributors communicate with their accounts in a number of ways. Often, the first time a retailer will hear about an upcoming release is through a monthly new release catalog that the distributor creates and sends to all its accounts. Labels/artists have the opportunity to advertise their new releases in this catalog (the

cost of which, of course, is charged back to you), through full-size
or fractional ads. These catalog ads have the following information for the benefit of the retailer:

- release date
- title and description of release
- album mini (thumbnail of record cover)
- main marketing points (press and radio plan, consumer
  advertising campaign, tour dates, etc.)
- SRLP (Suggested Retail List Price)
- UPC codes

Fig. 4.1. A mini from Hip Son's *Easygoing* release.
www.hipsonmusic.com

Promo Copies

You know those CDs you see with a hole through the bar code?
Those are promo CDs or "advances" that at one time were sent
to retailers, writers at press, or music directors at radio to help
build the buzz prior to an artist's proper release. Distributors
need advances in order to sell to buyers at retail. Advances
have a nasty habit of ending up in the used CD bin or for sale
online, but they are a necessary evil to engage retailers prior to a
release.

P.O.P. (Point of Purchase)

P.O.P. refers to marketing promo items that are used at retail
locations (the "point of purchase"). While some labels make some
pretty outrageous and costly P.O.P. items, traditionally typical
P.O.P.s would include:

- 11x17 retail/tour posters
- "white label" 4-track samplers
- sticker postcards with key album art
- 12x12 double-sided thin cardboard pieces with cover art for
  use in displays

COMMUNICATING WITH YOUR DISTRIBUTOR

As the marketing of a release unfolds, it is essential for the label to communicate updates and news to the distributor on a national and, particularly, regional basis. Remember, the distributor is reliant on the label to create and implement the marketing plan for an artist. The distributor reacts to news from a label, which it then filters through to retail.

INSIDER TIP: LABEL COMMUNICATION AND INVENTORY

Rykodisc was working on a record several years ago by a group of four female singer/songwriters from the Northeast who performed and recorded collectively as Voices on the Verge. Two of the four women had a moderate background at retail and press, but because the record was a live release recorded two years prior, the shipping, sales, and manufacturing projections were relatively low. The record initially was selling around what was projected (400 units a week), until NPR decided to do an interview. The piece was amazing—an excellent interview interspersed with music from the album. NPR broadcasted the piece nationally during evening drive time, and the record exploded! Sales went from 400 to close to 3,500 a week (with much of the sales coming from Amazon)! While we at the label were celebrating, the inventory manager at our distributor was tearing his hair out, as he did not have enough product to keep up with the demand. No one knew it would be so successful. Although Amazon ran out of product for two days, the situation could have been much worse if we had not alerted the inventory manager that this press hit was coming.

Typically, the sales department at a label is in day-to-day contact with the distributor, checking stock and sales, and working directly with the label's product manager on any retail updates or hot spots. Additionally, the product manager usually speaks with the national reps on a weekly or biweekly basis on a national conference call. The distribution reps are interested in the following information:

- **Tour:** *Very* important. Touring artists sell records. The regional sales reps want to know how the tour is going, what size venues the artist is playing, and when they are coming to their particular region. The rep takes this information to the retails, and if the retailer is low on product, would typically ask that they purchase enough to supply the expected demand of the tour.

- **Press:** Did *Rolling Stone* do a cover story? What national outlets are reviewing the record? What regional outlets are doing a spotlight on the artist to coincide with the tour dates?

- **Radio:** Who's on it? Is the record number 1 at WRAS in Atlanta? If so, Eric at Criminal needs to know about it so he can be sure he's covered.

- **NPR:** Is Teri Gross chatting with the artist on Fresh Air?
- **What else?** Internet, video, licensing news? Every bit of information helps!

One-Stops

What Is a "One-Stop"?

A *one-stop* is a wholesaler that provides retailers with the ability to purchase product offered from many separate distributors through one centralized place: a "one-stop shop" option. In theory, one-stops make the life of the retailer a little bit easier: time savings through consolidated buying options, and immediate shipping, easier accounting by working with one vendor instead of many, and reduced shipping costs. One-stops come in several varieties, from large national options like Super D and AEC (Alliance Entertainment Corporation) that work with thousands of indie retailers and major chains, to the niche one-stops like White Swan that primarily fulfill targeted alternative retailers such as new age bookstores.

One-stops differ from traditional distributors in a couple of ways. One-stops will do business with more-or-less anyone, and have more flexible terms in that they'll do credit cards, and C.O.D. orders. They also are more expensive to work with—retailers pay a premium for the luxury of the more favorable terms and quicker shipping.

While more expensive, traditional distribution provides retailers with a dedicated sales rep or expert on their product, better pricing, and the option of providing promos, P.O.P., and co-op to the retailers (which one-stops do not offer).

Summary

There are a number of different physical distribution options available for artists. While the larger national distributors require that artists have a substantial national following and a steady stream of income/releases, smaller regional distributors and "umbrella" groups are more willing to work with developing artists that have outgrown their ability to distribute music themselves. Unlike digital distribution, which is largely pain-free, some physical distribution policies (like returns, reserves, and other outdated fees) make it really tough for developing artists to succeed and thrive with physical distribution. Overall, it's important to remember that distribution follows marketing. If a developing artist has very little marketing happening and folks are not clamoring for the release, physical distribution might not be the best choice. Before soliciting distribution options, developing artists need to first cultivate a base. As this base grows out from regional to national, artists can then use physical distribution to then reach these folks who are already hip to your music through the other marketing efforts you are engaged in: touring, online, press, radio, etc.

Workshop

- What distribution model (major, independent owned by a major, true large national independent, regional independent, umbrella group) do you think would be the most appropriate for your music (or the music you plan to market), and why?

- What specific distributor would be the best choice, and why? Research specific bands that are currently distributed by this distributor, potential distribution fees, what stores this distributor works with, and if they are regional, where they distribute product. This may require a call to the offices of the distributor you choose.

5 | Marketing to Traditional Retail

Independent music retailers (the "mom and pop" stores of the world, as opposed to the "big box" retailers like Target and Wal-Mart) have been having a tough go at it over the past few years. Great artist-friendly independent stores, like Aron's and Rhino Records in L.A. and NYCD in New York City, have closed their doors over the past couple of years. Some studies claim that the number of stand-alone music retailers (meaning retailers that primarily sell music) is down from 5,000 a decade ago to around 2,500 today.

All this being said, the shrewd retailers that are adapting and evolving to this changing landscape are still making it, some with the best sales they've had in years. Retail (more specifically, independent retail) can still be counted on as the best supporters of up-and-coming artists. It's important for all artists to understand how retail works, what affects this outlet, and how you can use this resource to help further your marketing and sales goals.

SETTING THE STAGE: THE PROBLEMS WITH RETAIL, AND HOW SMART STORES ARE OVERCOMING THEM

The Difficulties in Physical Retail for Independents

It's easy to blame digital file sharing and the rise of legitimate online music retailers for physical retail's troubles. While they are definitely part of the problem, the entire picture is a bit more involved. Stand-alone music retailers have been fighting a number of battles for years. In addition to the rise of online music (legitimate and otherwise), the other major causes for retail's troubles are the high prices of CDs and competition from big-box retailers (which, while they sell music, are not really considered music stores).

Here's what's happening:

Low Margin / High CD Prices

The label and its distributors determine the suggested retail list price (SRLP) of a CD. Distributors sell the product to the retailers at 30 percent off the SRLP, which means that the best a retailer can do on a single CD and not lose money is this 30 percent ($11.29 on a $15.98 CD, for example). Because of the marketing effort the label has to put into a new artist's release to even get buy-in from the retailers (radio promotion, press, advertising, co-op), it's simply not cost-effective for a label that is undertaking a national marketing campaign on behalf of a new artist to permanently lower the CD price to something respectable, like $9.99. Although there are deals and sales—and some labels will drop the CD prices on new artists and take a loss (with the hopes of building a base to sell the next record at full price), it's really not an option for labels and distributors to drop CD prices across the board, with the current financial responsibilities required to market music. This ultimately affects the consumer, who seeks music elsewhere.

Big Box Competition

Wal-Mart and Best Buy are two of the largest music retail outlets in the U.S. However, they have limited shelf space and rarely stock a title that is projected to sell less than 100,000 units.

The difficulty that independent retail has been having with their larger competitors is twofold.

First, because these outlets really make their money from better margin items like appliances and housewares, they are not concerned with the small margin that music releases produce. To them, CDs are loss leaders. That means that their function is to lure people into the store in hopes that they will also buy higher ticket items like refrigerators or flat-screen TVs. Big-box retailers have the right to charge whatever they want on music releases, and they have the leverage to price new releases at or below cost. Because they are less concerned about their margin, big-box retailers can afford to sell for $12 the same Smashing Pumpkins record that an independent retailer might have listed at $15.98.

Second, because major labels realize that a substantial percentage of their sales are coming from these two outlets, the labels provide big-box stores with exclusive releases to increase their buy-in. A good example of this is the Best Buy–exclusive Forty Licks DVD from the Rolling Stones. Independent retailers had a fit because they could not sell it. The Boston-based indie chain Newbury Comics even threatened to remove the Rolling Stones back catalog from their shelves. In late 2007, Reprise, the Smashing Pumpkins' label at the time, decided to release different exclusive releases of their new record to three large big-box retailers: Target, Best Buy, and iTunes (the largest online distributor, and third largest music store out there). While Billy Corgan (lead singer and guitarist) has done some really great things for his community online (offering demos and unreleased records online for free), this move alienated his fan base and seriously upset the independent retailers.

INSIDER TIP: HOW THE INDEPENDENT RETAILERS REALLY FEEL ABOUT BIG-BOX EXCLUSIVES

Eric Levin founded Atlanta's Criminal Record, one of the nation's most respected independent retailers, in 1989. In 2002, Eric formed the Alliance of Independent Media Stores, a trade group representing thirty stores nationally. Read an e-mail that Eric sent out to his retail coalition partners about the Pumpkins' decision, and the independent retailers' battles with big-box retailers.

What's wrong with Billy Corgan? The Smashing Pumpkins didn't even play at Live Earth. It seems like some of the indie record stores and our customers out there felt a little screwed by the rollout of their new release. I even read about it on the interweb.

Mighty A.I.M.S. retailer Stinkweeds in Tempe, AZ, received this letter from one Smashing Pumpkins fan:

"In early 2006, the Red Hot Chili Peppers, having recorded a glut of new material, decided that a three-disc Stadium Arcadium would be too much to release at once. So they devised a plan: release a two-disc set, but release the extra songs as bonus tracks. These bonus tracks would be dispersed as chain exclusives. Each retail outlet, including the big-box retailers and (supposedly) a smattering of indie stores, would get a different bonus track. There would have been something like twelve bonus tracks, or twelve official versions of the album. Anthony Kiedis promoted this as a service to all the different stores that carried his product."

Thankfully, they never went through with it. Instead of servicing the chains, what it really would have done is rip off the fans. Music collecting is something people can get really passionate about. I once knew a guy with over 200 Björk CDs, and this was in 1996, when Björk only had two albums out. Likewise, RHCP still has some old-school, hardcore fans, but asking anyone to spend roughly $200 for all the new tracks is simply too much. The move would have either disappointed real fans who would never hear all those new songs, or it would have driven them to the file-sharing networks.

Having not thought through any of this, Billy Corgan, in his infinite hubris, decided that he'd pull the same stunt with four versions of Zeitgeist, three with bonus tracks. The versions with bonus tracks are available at a handful of global chains only, each with its own bonus track. Indie record stores such as Stinkweeds will not have the bonus tracks for sale.

This is really nothing new. Many obscure tracks are only published overseas, while EU artists like A Band of Bees and Stina Nordenstam have bonus tracks in North America, to encourage sales of an unknown, foreign artist. So sometimes, we benefit from this. Not only that, but the Pumpkins usually bundle and re-release their b-sides and rarities ("Pisces Iscariot," "The Aeroplane Flies High," "Judas O," etc.), so the tracks will probably surface again.

Does Corgan think you'll buy four versions of "Zeitgeist?" Probably not. But he is encouraging you to spend your Pumpkins money at the big-box retailers instead of their friendly neighborhood record store. And he probably got a ton of cash up-front. But this move signifies the desire to move music fans away from establishments dedicated to feeding the need for new and experimental music. It encourages moving business to large-scale retailers who sell CDs at low or negative profit in order to get you into the store to buy high-margin items such as software and display accessories. Their shareholders can't handle the financial risk of stocking new and unproven music.

In a capitalist society, your dollar is a vote. That dollar says, "I support the practices of this business. Please continue." Therefore, your music dollar at Best Buy is a vote for unknowledgeable clerks. Your music dollar at Target is a vote for two aisles of Top 40 and 1970s funk comps. "Hey, Wal-Mart! Please, give us more censorship and Toby Keith records! Here's my $12.88 for the cause!" If everybody keeps buying CDs at Wal-Mart, soon enough, that will be all we have left. However, your music dollar at a local independent record store will— guess what—help fund the development of independent music. If you choose to buy "Zeitgeist," please, choose wisely.

In addition to the big-box retailers, there are also regional and national chains that compete with independent retailers. Trans World Entertainment operates over 800 music retail locations nationwide. Their stores include f.y.e. (primarily mall locations), Coconuts, Wherehouse, Strawberries, Specs, and Planet Music (all freestanding stores). These stores, while competitors of independent retail, are less of a threat to indie retail, as they don't have the leverage to offer music releases at or under cost, like the big-box retailers. All the buying for these separate stores happens at the main Trans World office level, and there is very little room for any point-of-purchase items. Like Wal-Mart and Best Buy, these stores are more interested in top sellers from major labels than helping regional independent artists and smaller labels.

THE IMPORTANCE OF THE INDEPENDENT RETAILER AND RETAIL COALITIONS

Unlike the chains and the big-box guys, those that are responsible for managing and buying music at independent retail usually have a great handle on the local music scene, and are tied in to local venues and print publications. They've read the show reviews and know if folks have been asking about a specific local band. Many of these stores are also part of larger regional or national coalitions, which speak to each other on a regular basis about what's selling, what is under the radar but about to pop, and promotional strategies. The smart independent retailer, who is adapting to the evolving retail industry, is key to the success of an artist, both independent and those signed to a label.

Benefits of Independent Retailers

The independent retailer works to break new artists on a regional level. While independent retailers are as interested in making money as Wal-Mart's stockholders, they are much more open to helping out a regional band. Independent retailer owners and buyers have the ability to promote what they want and where, and while much of these spaces at a retailer location are tied up with co-op, there are areas in the store, listening posts, or even the in-store sound system that is completely up to the store's employees. Plus, artists that call out independent retail locations while playing in town ("We have our latest release here at the show, but for an exclusive EP, check out Newbury Comics!") earn special points with indie retail.

More Defined Customer Base. There's not really a defined demographic that shop for music at Best Buy or Target (not that many artists have the ability to market their releases at these locations anyway). But indie retail is very demographic-centered. Bull Moose, a great independent chain store in New Hampshire and Maine, has a number of stores that each specialize in different music: hard rock/metal, indie, classic rock, jazz etc. Independent retail allows artists and labels to more effectively target their fans by selling their music to folks that want to buy it.

Consignment. Don't have a distribution deal? No problem! Although consignment can be tricky (we'll discuss this soon), it's a great way to get your music out to your fans that may have missed your last show (where you have your CD for sale, of course).

Work Hand in Hand with Lifestyle Outlets. Indie retailers work closely with local restaurants, bars, coffee shops, etc. to promote artist performances as well as listening parties.

Many indies are also part of regional and national retail coalitions. Many of the best indie retailers in the country are part of larger coalitions that span regionally or nationally. The two largest and most effective coalitions are CIMS (Coalition of Independent Music Stores, envisioned by Terry Currier in 1994); and AIMS (Association of Independent Media Stores, founded by Eric Levin out of Atlanta, GA). The coalitions provide a number of benefits for artists and labels: a centralized source of information about each store, a centralized way to book co-op advertising and positioning regionally, and a barometer of what artists and music are doing well nationally at the indies.

INTERVIEW: ERIC LEVIN, FOUNDER OF
CRIMINAL RECORDS

Is part of the idea of your retail coalition to have a unified front to battle the big-box retailers?

I wouldn't really call it a unified front; it's more of a one-call-does-it-all type of thing. For a label or a band with a new project, without a coalition they'd have to make thirty different calls to thirty different retailers and learn and deal with, in my case, thirty different programs to promote their release. We sell listening posts, we sell video posts, and we do it efficiently. So if someone wants to do thirty of those with the stores I represent in my coalition, they can call me, and for the same price of dealing with the individual stores one-on-one, they can take care of it all with one call and they're done. The coalition has added a convenience to the labels that has allowed them to do their job more efficiently. That's really the basis of it. We share the revenue, which is fantastic, and all the stores get a check, which will keep the doors open at some stores, and go into the retirement account of others. But what is really cool is the communication between all the stores. Our listserv is always buzzing with questions, like "What are you selling your t-shirts for?" or "What do you guys think about the idea of selling sheet music?"

So you can see what works for other stores, and then try it out for yourself.

I might be friendly with other retailers in my local area, but I'm not going to call them up and ask them a business question. But the folks in my coalition—I ask them stuff all the time. Plus I've made some of the best friends I've ever had through this. When I travel, I get to see my friends. And there's a little bit of healthy competition between us. I want my displays to be awesome because when I send my e-newsletter out, I know the coalition folks are going to be looking at them. That competition, plus the camaraderie, plus the questions I can have answered, have made Criminal Records way better. I have to think it is the same thing for the others.

HOW SMART INDEPENDENTS ARE COMPETING IN THIS ENVIRONMENT

It's clear that many independent stores are having a difficult time adjusting to the new music economy. However, as we mentioned, there are a number of retailers that are surviving, thriving, and still serving as a viable outlet for labels and independent artists. Here's what's happening.

Diversification

Diversification is major. It's important for music retailers to be more than a destination for just music fans. In order to compete, they have to be more of a lifestyle destination. In addition to music, the nimble independent retailers sell t-shirts, DVDs, tchotchkes, concert posters, lava lamps, shoes, coffee. These sorts of items not only give consumers another reason to come into the store but also provide a wider margin than CDs.

Specialization

Another key to independent retailers success is specialization. Other Music in New York City is a great example of a store that has found a niche within the indie music community. Their buyers are cutting edge, and fans of unusual and rare releases can be guaranteed that they'll find something amazing at the store.

Used CDs

One advantage that independents have over chain retailers or big-box retailers is that they offer used CDs for sale. The profit margin is better on used CDs, which helps to offset the lack of margin for new CDs. While this practice doesn't really overtly help artists and labels, it does increase foot traffic into the store, and brings more visibility to new releases.

Vinyl

Vinyl is coming back! Vinyl sales doubled in 2007, rising from three million to six million units sold, with indie stores being the primary source of LPs in recent years.

Deeper Catalog

Independent retailers have the ability to stock deeper catalog titles than big-box retailers, who are focused on more "vanilla" best sellers.

More Knowledgeable Staff

For the discerning music fan, there is nothing like talking with a sales associate that can recommend music to you based on your particular taste. The employees at the independents are complete music junkies, unlike chains or big-box retailers.

CONSIGNMENT AND PRICING CONSIDERATIONS

The easiest (and preferred) way for artists and labels to get their music into a retailer is through a music distributor. Retailers are in contact with their distributors all the time, and placing an order with them is simple. However, for artists and labels that do not yet have a relationship with a distributor, many independent retailers offer consignment as an option to get CDs in the store.

What Is Consignment?

In the music retail world, consignment is the act of providing physical product to a store for them to sell. But instead of paying you upfront, as they would in a traditional distribution agreement, the retailer doesn't pay until the product sells.

How It Works

Consignment details are different from retailer to retailer, and some indies won't do out-of-state consignment. With others, you have to submit a consignment request in person, and some don't even accept consignment at all. But with all indie record stores, you have to earn the right to get placement and product in the store. Many stores will do a one-piece consignment purchase for three months, and if that piece moves, the store will then do a larger buy-in. Stores need finished product with artwork (not CDRs), and a bar code helps as well if you want to track the sales through SoundScan.

How to Price Your CD

Many indie retailers will give you the option to price your consigned CD at whatever price you like. However, just like when you decide to price out your merch, you have to consider what you want this release to do for you. Is it a tool to get folks to the gigs? It is a way to promote yourself? Is it an income stream?

RETAIL MARKETING OPPORTUNITIES AND RESOURCES

Once you've got your music into a retailer through traditional distribution means or via consignment, many indie stores provide several options to help you move your music back off the shelves. All the segments in the music industry work off one another in a symbiotic relationship, and retail is no exception. Independent retail is very sensitive to external marketing (radio, Internet and physical press, lifestyle outlets, and live shows in particular), and many retailers work closely with these outlets to help promote new releases.

There are a lot of tools that retail marketers use to help communicate with indie stores and take advantage of any internal marketing they offer. All record labels have a retail database that lists every important store in the country by geographic location, tracks who buys for what genre at that store, lists available in-store possibilities, and details the external outlets that affect sales at the stores (i.e., specific radio stations or press outlets). An effective retail marketing department at a label would plan visibility at the indie stores prior to the record's release (based on projected popular geographic regions laid out in the initial marketing plan), and would also follow any other significant external marketing visibility as the marketing plan develops with internal store-level visibility.

In-Stores

In-store performances can be initiated by the artist/label or the store itself. If a store is really into the release and you are diligent about keeping them up to date with tour plans in the area, the store may request that you stop by prior to your date.

In-stores are expensive. The back-end equipment alone could run a few hundred dollars to rent, if you don't have your own available, and the store/distributor would usually expect that some co-op advertising be taken out to support the event. But an in-store has the potential of revving up a particular market and showing a retailer that you support their efforts. Additionally, the retailer will also place a larger order with you/your distributor to cover the additional foot traffic and fans that they expect to come see the in-store performance.

INSIDER TIP: PULLING OFF A SUCCESSFUL IN-STORE

In-stores are not to be taken lightly. I've seen some amazing ones with incredible traffic (a new release artist pulling more than a hundred fans for a record release in-store in Boston) and some catastrophic duds (that same artist playing in New Hampshire to the store manager, myself, and one person who happened to be browsing the store at 3:00 p.m. on a Tuesday). Always take into account location, timing, and potential fans in the area before ever agreeing to do an in-store. Also, with the online tools now available to communicate directly and immediately with your fan base, there really is no excuse for not letting all of your fans within a hundred mile radius know that you have an in-store coming up. Be proactive about bringing fans!

Price and Positioning/Co-Op/P.O.P. Items

If you are with a distributor, it's likely that the distributor would have already worked out co-op visibility ahead of time, and is also in constant communication with the retailers about current marketing initiatives you or your label are doing. If you're working on your own, it makes sense to connect with the retailer yourself and follow up with flyers, postcards, and especially tour posters to support your other efforts. If you are playing in town and already supporting your date with tour posters (more on this soon), it's very easy to ship the same posters over to the independent retailer and tag the upcoming gig.

COVER ART AND EFFECTIVE PACKAGING

Cover Art

Marketing folks have to be careful about graphic designers. While a designer might have a completely amazing idea for the cover art that requires one to know the Aramaic language in order to read the artist name and title, marketing has to put themselves in the shoes of the retailer and the retail environment when thinking about the cover art. If you are a relatively new artist, it is likely you will not have a bin card—the plastic card that retailers use in the aisles of CDs to identify the artist, which stands about 2 inches above the top of the rows of CDs and allows folks who are browsing for a particular artist to find their section immediately. More likely, your CD will be placed in the "lettered" section of the retailer (as in, the general "P" category if your band is called the P. James Magic Show). Folks tend to blow through these lettered sections pretty quickly, and if your name is not immediately visible on the CD cover, someone who is genuinely looking for it can easily miss your release. Additionally, if you think about how CDs sit in the bin and how folks flip through them, the most visible area on the CD cover is the top third. Again, you want to make it as easy as possible for folks to find your music. If you are spending time and money marketing your music, do yourself a favor and make the actual product easy to find. It also makes sense to consider the fact that your cover art will be used in places outside of the physical product, such as online and in print as a "mini" or a thumbnail. If your title is tiny on the physical product, it will be even smaller online!

INSIDER TIP: GRAPHIC DESIGNERS ARE NOT MARKETING EXPERTS

Graphic designers tend to call out the Beatles' *Sgt. Peppers* and Pink Floyd's *Dark Side of the Moon* as records that do not follow the above cover art rules. Don't be fooled by this argument! If David Gilmore or Paul McCartney are in your band, then I would say do whatever you like. But for 99 percent of the artists out there, you need to make your release easier to find, not harder.

Other Helpful Packaging Elements

Rykodisc, the former large independent label (now owned by Warner Music Group), invented the spine cap—the area at the top of the CD that lists the title and UPC code. Everyone at Ryko referred to this as the "obi," which is a Japanese word referring to the top-most sash worn with various styles of Japanese clothing. The obi, or spine cap, is a great way to add additional visibility to your release, and because it comes down ¾ of an inch on the front and rear cover, it allows you to place marketing copy (a great quote or description of your music) right on the release. You can also print on the rear side of the obi, which is space that can be used to list additional releases you have.

The obi on the Pretenders *Break Up The Concrete* contains live seeds, as you can see in in figure 5.1.

(a) Front

(b) Rear

Fig. 5.1. Obi (a) Front and (b) Rear

SOUNDSCAN: WHAT IT IS AND WHY IT MATTERS

Nielsen Broadcasting is best known as the company that rates the popularity of television programs. In addition to TV, the company is also diversified in several music entertainment properties, and is the owner of *Billboard* magazine, as well as SoundScan.

SoundScan is an online service that tracks the sale of music and video releases. Any music product that carries a bar code is eligible to be tracked by SoundScan, if the retailer elects to report its sales to SoundScan. Although this is no longer the case, Newbury Comics elected not to report their sales to SoundScan for years, as they thought that their competitors could use the information and negatively affect their own sales. Almost all of the major independent stores, as well as the chains and big-box retailers, report their sales to SoundScan. The service reports sales every Tuesday morning. Anytime you hear information about the top-selling records or top-selling singles for any period of time, you can be sure that this information was provided by SoundScan. In addition to sales produced by retail outlets, touring artists can also report their venue sales themselves to the service by faxing in reporting documents.

INSIDER TIP: SELLING YOUR CD AT SHOWS

When Prince toured to support his *Musicology* release in 2005, every person that bought a ticket to his show got a free copy of his record. This was a great way to build word-of-mouth buzz on his new record by getting it directly into the hands of his fans. Further, every copy he gave out was considered a trackable venue sale by SoundScan. These sales helped to vault Prince's new record to the top of the charts, and produced even more publicity and word-of-mouth visibility. Other artists, including Lindsay Buckingham from Fleetwood Mac, are also using the technique to get new music out to their hard-core fan base.

SoundScan is a great tool for the music marketers. The service breaks sales out in a number of ways to help marketers decide where to put their marketing dollars, including: independent/chain sales, online vs. physical sales, and most importantly, geography. Keep in mind, though: the service is pricey for the casual music marketing maven. Pricing plans can be worked out here: sales@soundscan.com.

Why SoundScan Matters

SoundScan is one of the most effective tools that marketing folks (and artists that have the cash for a subscription) have to judge the success of their physical sales. At a label, the first thing the marketing department does on Tuesday morning is check SoundScan, and then talk about the past week's sales in their marketing meeting Tuesday afternoon. Marketing can then see how specific campaigns or visibility like a radio appearance, press hit, or live show has affected sales by region. Because all music-marketing plans are fluid documents, if the marketing team sees an unexpected spike in sales in a particular area, they can dedicate more resources there to keep the wheel spinning.

For independent artists, SoundScan can be used for the same marketing purposes. But over and above any marketing information it offers, SoundScan sales can become part of the artist's overall story. If any artist is interested in gaining the attention of a distributor or record label, a great SoundScan sales story is a valuable tool. Labels love the idea of signing artists that have momentum and can prove that they have a dedicated following in certain areas.

Summary

Although CD sales are in decline, independent retailers can be a great partner for developing artists. As an alternative to the homogenization of music at the big-box stores, many indies have a deeper, more varied catalog and a greater ability to promote local and independent artists. Indies are also often flexible about consignment opportunities and pricing, and react well to artists that help to move their product off the shelves.

Workshop

Visit an independent retailer and a big-box retailer, and consider the following:

- What differences do you see in the P.O.P. between the two outlets?

- What CDs do you see highlighted in the endcaps of each? What are some of the marketing reasons for choosing one endcap over another?

- What are the differences in price between the independent retailer and the national chain on new releases? Can you tell by comparing the two if the big-box retailer is selling below cost?

- Talk to the music manager at the independent and big-box retailers, and report back on the visibility options that are available to you.

- Are there any lifestyle marketing options associated with the independent retailer?

- What form of P.O.P. does the independent prefer?

- Does the independent retailer have consignment options? If so, what are the details?

- What other ways does the independent retailer highlight local or independent label artists?

6

Online, Mobile, and Video Marketing

The Internet has completely changed the overall marketing picture for developing musicians. It's been said that there are now more online artist service companies than there are artists! From online resources designed to help you distribute and sell your music, to resources that help you form and coordinate online street teams, license your music, gain visibility through contests, or a million other activities, the Internet provides musicians with a cost-effective way to get their music heard by more folks than ever before. And unlike a lot of marketing, it's all trackable. You can immediately see what is working and what isn't. The downside is that there is more "noise" online than ever before, too. The Internet provides a voice for everyone, and the trick is to find a way to cut through the clutter and not just market yourself online, but market yourself online intelligently. As Heath Ledger's Joker famously said in *The Dark Knight*, "It's all part of the plan."

In this chapter, we'll discuss your online marketing campaign: getting a site together that attracts and engages your fans, making sure folks can find it through the search engines, effective outfacing online marketing techniques, online tools that can help you coordinate and maintain your community, and making the most of video.

IT ALL STARTS AT HOME

Successful Internet marketing is more than just having a MySpace page, more than compiling and sending out update e-mails to your list, and more than throwing videos up on YouTube. While all these outfacing initiatives are great and should be part of your complete online campaign, a solid Internet campaign begins at home, with your own site.

Artists whose sole online visibility is their MySpace page may be making a fundamental mistake. MySpace and other social networking sites do provide a basic way for musicians to get online visibility, but they lack the creativity and customization ability that your own site can provide. Your job online is to nurture a relationship with your potential fans. If you don't, there are a million other bands and sites that these folks can check out. It's vital that you play to your strengths on your site, and present yourself in the best (and most creative) possible way.

The main components all effective Web sites need to address are:

- Usability
- Content
- Effective use of media
- Making your site an interactive community

A Broad Overview on Usability

Too many folks set up their Web sites without keeping in mind the number 1 fundamental of Web design: usability. It's easy to get carried away with extraneous bells and whistles that may be visually interesting, but without a clear purpose and solid navigation, folks will tend to get confused and leave. This is what usability is all about. First and foremost, a Web site must be functional. It must have a clear purpose and it must be easy for users to navigate.

Here's a quick hit list of usability considerations for laying out your site:

Do

- **Make the navigation as clear as possible.** Some artists design their site with pop-up navigation and cleverly hidden links. This may look cool, but potential fans that are finding out about you for the first time are not going to want to take the time to figure out how to operate your site.

- **Make the purpose of your site as clear as possible.** Your band's logo or name should be up top, in a font that is consistent with how the name is presented on your CD or other merch you make. You want folks to know that this is the band's official Web site, not a fan site.

- **Stay true to the focus of the site.** What is most important for your users to know? Are you constantly touring? If so, the tour button on your nav should be really prominent, and your homepage should have your tour dates front and center. Is the main purpose of your site to sell merch? If so, then this should be highlighted.

- **Make it easy.** Allow folks to access information, sign up for your newsletter, post on your blog, or buy your merch with the fewest amount of clicks possible. You want to make it as easy as possible for your fans to interact with you.

Don't

- **Be copy heavy on the site.** Folks don't read online; they skim. Keep your descriptive copy short! New users generally spend thirty seconds on your homepage. Encapsulate what you do in as few words as possible.

- **Use large graphics that take a long time to load.** By the time the graphic has finished loading, your user will be gone.

- **Force people to watch a video or listen to music when they show up on the site.** There are opposing views on this, but my opinion is that many folks are already listening to music through speakers or headphones when they are online. It's a drag to have to turn off the music or sound from a video when they show up on your site. You need to give your users a reason to come back to the site, not a reason to stay away.

Note: There are many resources out there on Web design and usability. A really good starting point is Steve Krug's book *Don't Make Me Think*. Learn more about Steve and his usability ideas on his Web site: www.sensible.com.

INSIDER TIP: GRAMMAR RESOURCES

There are a lot of great online resources you can use to be sure your grammar is squeaky clean. *The Chicago Manual of Style Online* is a great searchable resource for any pesky grammar questions you have. The *Grammar Girl* podcast (one of the top-listened-to podcasts!) is another great resource.

Content

To build an effective online community, you need to give fans a reason to continue to come back to your site. Over and above all other retention techniques, regularly posted content is the most effective way to get folks to revisit your site on a consistent basis. Outdated news is a sure sign that nothing is happening with your band, which is the last thing you want your fans to think. Here are a couple of easy ways to keep your Web site fresh.

Volume and Frequency. Not only is it a good idea to constantly update the content of your site from a user perspective, but the search engines also favor sites that are constantly changing. (It proves your site is relevant and active.) Search engines also like to see sites with more than ten pages.

Blog. Fans want to be part of the conversation, not just read about events. A blog on your site is an easy way to add current content, keep your fans up-to-date, and involve them in the conversation. Touring or recording blogs are great. Letting fans know how the tour is going, where you are headed, who you are playing with, and what songs you're playing not only accomplishes the "frequency" aspect of an effective Web site, it also personalizes what you are doing and makes your fans feel like they are part of a smaller community. Same thing if you are in the studio. Let your fans know what you are doing and where you are at in the process so that you can build anticipation for the release. As a bonus, you can reward your fans that are keeping up-to-date with you with a "demo" version of a song you are working on. Joseph Arthur, an amazing singer-songwriter living in Brooklyn, keeps a really creative "Notes from the Road" blog on his site. It's a blog written in poetic form and sometimes updated daily!

Micro-blogging. Micro-blogging is blogging lite. Rather than full-content posts, micro blogs are typically 140 characters max. Considered by some to be the evolution of blogging, micro-blogging is a great way to keep folks up-to-date with your activities in an easy-to-digest manner. Currently Twitter (www.twitter.com, a free service, at the moment) is the leader of the micro-blog services.

Visuals. Archive everything, but only post the most professional looking and interesting visual content you have. Images are an exercise in branding, and if you consider yourself a serious band, you need your images to represent that. This rule also applies to:

Professionally Written Content. Punctuation is important! Writing copy for your Web site is not the same as writing an instant message or a text message. Your Web site is your online calling card. Don't distract site visitors with bad grammar. It's much more important for folks to leave your site with solid information than with the knowledge that you don't know the difference between "your" and "you're." Also, the Web robots from the search engines apparently prefer well-written content too! Who knew there were so many critics out there!

External Content. There's no shame in editorializing content created by someone else. The fact is that there is no shortage of major music-related news floating around these days. If there happens to be a lull in your band's activity, post some thoughts on a current music event that affects your band, or some comments on the state of the industry. Have an opinion on mechanical royalty rates paid out for online sales? Post your thoughts in your news section!

INSIDER TIP: EXAMPLES OF GOOD AND BAD WEB SITES

GOOD DESIGN:

The Chemical Brothers: www.thechemicalbrothers.com/home/

The Chemical Brothers Web site is a good example of Web design, usability, and interesting content that will work to convert potential fans and give them a reason to return back to the site. The band name and their logo is top left (where most users eyes intuitively go to when they first visit a Web site), and the navigation is very obvious, both in placement, size, and naming conventions. The Chemical Brothers are also effectively using technology to engage their fans via the Google Earth promotion on their homepage, which fans can make their own short clip or photograph on the theme of the Chemical Brothers new single, upload the work via the Chemical Brothers Web site to Google Earth, and tag it to their exact global location. The site is easy to get around, visually appealing, and offers fans plenty of ways to get involved with the band.

BAD DESIGN:

Bjork: www.bjork.com/

I'm a big fan of Bjork's music, but her current Web site is a conundrum to me. The site is very difficult to navigate, as the navigation bar is hidden in small text on the left hand side of the page, and the tabs are not named in a way that is immediately recognizable as links to information that I would be interested in learning more about. The main headers on the homepage are also very difficult to read at first glance as they are in 7-point font! If a fan powers through the poor initial design there is some good information within the site, but the casual user will most likely quit the process in frustration before they have the opportunity to dig deeper.

Effective Use of Media

There is a quote, generally attributed to Elvis Costello, "Writing about music is like dancing about architecture." Anyone that has ever written a band's press release would almost certainly agree. The most effective way to turn someone onto your music is not by telling them about it, it's by having them listen to it. Here are a few techniques for online media that I'd like to recommend:

Offer Full Tracks. Providing a thirty-second stream doesn't cut it anymore. You want to be welcoming to your fans, not make them think they can only hear the full song if they buy it.

Create a Podcast. An easy way to get potential fans interested in you and your music is by creating a podcast. Podcasts are essentially just MP3 files, and of course, the topics you can discuss are limitless. There are a number of free or cheap options you can use to get started with creating a podcast. (Apple's GarageBand program is very user friendly and easy to use.)

There are also some great online tools out there for hosting media on your site. One easy-to-use tool is the Wimpy player. The Wimpy player allows you to stream full songs from your homepage in a non-obtrusive player (which you can skin yourself to make it match your site). Learn more: www.wimpyplayer.com.

Make Your Site a Community

Ten years ago, a typical band's Web site consisted of static items designed to present information to potential fans: a bio, photos, press quotes, maybe a streaming track, and a link to join the label's mailing list.

As Lawrence Lessig (founder of Creative Commons, a nonprofit that advocates copyright reform) says, we are now living in a "read-write"—not a read-only—society. Folks now want to be able to contribute to the conversation and interact with the content, not just read the content. Successful Web sites are now more about providing a platform for users to interact. Blog postings soliciting comments is an easy first step, but more engaging activities, such as contests where you provide tracks for your fans to remix your music, are even better.

INSIDER TIP: ONLINE STREET TEAM RESOURCES

While it is still important to have a physical street team component to help promote new releases (and in particular shows!), a number of online services have emerged over the past few years that use the power of the Internet and social networking to empower online "street teams." Companies like www.reverbnation.com and www. fancorps.com provide artists with street team management software that they can use to organize targeted campaigns, distribute banners, and automatically track the number of impressions, click-throughs, and placements throughout the campaign.

Make Your Content Viral

One of the best examples of a viral campaign I have seen over the past few years was one designed to support Bob Dylan's newest *Greatest Hits* package. It's a great take on Dylan's iconic *Subterranean Homesick Blues* video, where instead of Dylan holding large white cards with phrases from his song written on them, the animators of the video have provided a way for users to write their own phrases on the cards, with 1960s-era Dylan himself presenting his fans' personalized messages. The video ends with a promo on the release of Dylan's new record.

This campaign accomplishes the two main functions of an effective viral campaign: making the campaign so interesting and fun that I have to send it to my friends, and getting the message (in this case, the new record announcement) out to as many people as possible.

SEO: MAKING YOUR SITE POP!

SEO (search engine optimization) is a term used to describe activities related to the goal of having your site appear high in the search phrase return in Google, Yahoo, MSN, and so on. There are both paid and free (or organic) ways to do this. It's a true art, and people that can do this well are in high demand. Once you've got your content in order, and you're confident that you're providing your fans and users with reasons to come back to your site, the next step is to get SEO happening so people can find you online through a simple search. It's important to understand, however, that SEO only improves your odds for a high search return; it does not make any guarantees.

How can you be sure that someone searching for "Death metal in the Chicago area" will find your band, for example? The search engines use a complex, ever-changing algorithm to make a user's search results as relevant as possible. There are a number of factors that go into how the search engines return their results, including how "trusted" a site is, how long it has been online, how many folks are linking to it, how often the content is updated, how the content is displayed and tagged, and so on.

Creating an effective SEO strategy is similar to playing guitar: it takes a short time to learn the basics, but a long time to master. Entire books are dedicated to the subject, but the following information provides some fundamentals that every music marketer should be aware of to make their site as "search engine friendly" as possible.

The search engines use "spiders" or "robots" that constantly crawl the Internet and catalog all the content on every site online. These robots look for several main things on your site to determine what the site is about and how relevant it is:

Site Copy

The words that you use to describe your music, band, or label are very important to your search engine rankings. Your copy has to be effective in conveying your message to those who are already aware of your site, but you also have to be thinking about what the potential fans who you want to visit your site are typing into the search engines (these words are known as keywords, and we'll talk more about them soon). To paraphrase a terribly old marketing adage, "You want to fish where the fishes are."

An Example

Say you are an artist that specializes in writing, performing, and selling children's music. Your target market is likely made up of parents who are searching online for music to play for their kids. When preparing copy for your Web site, you need to think about the most popular words and phrases that these parents will use when they do their Web search. "Children's music" seems like the perfect phrase to use in your copy, but in fact, the phrase "kid's music" is actually a more popularly searched phrase, and should be liberally incorporated into the site to take advantage of the higher search volume. But remember, you are writing for humans, not search engines. Don't go overboard!

INSIDER TIP: FREE WEB ANALYTICS TOOL

There are some free online resources that can help you determine keyword popularity. A popular free resource is currently provided by Wordtracker (which also offers a more robust paid version). www.wordtracker.com

Metadata

The copy you use to describe yourself in the HTML code on your site (Metadata) is another factor for the search engines. This code is invisible to the user but searchable by Web crawlers. Metadata is broken out into three main categories.

Title. The title metadata is the copy that is seen at the top of your browser window when you visit a site. (For example, Berklee Press's title on the homepage is currently BerkleePress: Music Instruction Books, CDs, and DVDs.) This copy sets the stage for the search engines, and needs to be as relevant as possible with that particular page's mission. The copy in the title area is given a heavier weight by the search engines than other Metadata copy.

Title metadata should also change with every page to best describe the function of the page. For example, if you have a page dedicated to touring, be sure to adjust your title metadata to reflect that, as this example shows up top:

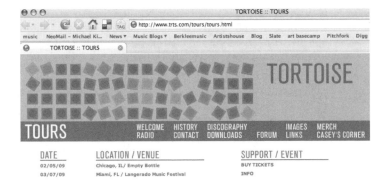

Fig. 6.1. Tortoise. Tours metadata on top.

This way, if someone is searching for your band's tour dates, the search engines can determine that this page is a valid page that should come up high in results.

Description. Although possibly not used by the robots to rank your site, the description metadata is important nonetheless, as it is the copy that appears under your Web site name in search results. Again, this should be rich in popular keywords, but written for the benefit of a human, not a search-engine spider. For example, Bob Dylan's Columbia-run Web site has the description of "Bob Dylan's Official Website on Columbia Records."

Keywords. Metadata keywords are strictly for the benefit of search engines. Once you have determined the most popular keywords and phrases to describe your site or your band (including misspellings!), you should be sure that they are all represented in the keyword metadata. There's no hard and fast rule about the quantity of acceptable keywords, but don't overdo it. Conventional wisdom says that a dozen keywords is more than enough, although there is indeed no hard and fast rule. Columbia obviously feels the more the better; here are the keywords that they are currently using for Dylan's site.

> *Bob Dylan, Robert Allen Zimmerman, Robert Dylan, no direction home, blowing in the wind, blowin in the wind, the times they are a changin, love and theft, modern times, like a rolling stone, chimes of freedom, mr. tambourine man, knockin on heaven's door, all along the watchtower, the band, masked and anonymous, the essential bob dylan, the freewheelin bob dylan, blonde on blonde, theme time radio hour, XM radio, singer songwriter, guitar, folk music, rock, the shadow blasters, the golden chords, Jakob Dylan, Martin Scorsese, Columbia Records, SONY BMG music entertainment*

Header Text. Effective header text (the copy you or your coder uses for the <H1> and <H2> headers on your site) should be another consideration for the robots. It's important to use effective keywords here as well, with the understanding that robots pay more attention to header text than paragraph (<P>) text. Text at the top of the page is also weighted higher than the text below!

Alt Text. Currently, robots can't read images. It's important to note that if you use a lot of images or graphics on your site, you should use "alt text" (which the robots can read) to describe these images.

So where do you put this information?

If you are coding your own HTML on your Web site (my hat is off to you), you can certainly hand-code all of this info in. If you are using a Web program like Dreamweaver, you can choose the Insert function and drop in the appropriate info that way, too. But if you have hired a coder to create your site, it's important that you communicate this information to whomever you are working with. It may sound difficult and abstract, but adding metadata information to your site is actually one of the easier things to accomplish online!

Links to Your Site and Links out to Other Like-Minded Sites

It might seem counterintuitive to provide links to other Web sites, but the more active, involved, and connected your site is with others, the better your chances of returning higher on search queries. Consider Wikipedia, currently the ninth most visited site on the Web. Wikipedia is about as optimized as you can get. It not only links out to hundreds of thousands of relevant sites; it also has an incredible amount of sites linking back to it. Consider creating a page on your site dedicated to similar bands, labels you like, the distributor you work with, and so on. Request a link from them in exchange. Doing so will raise your visibility with the search engines, as mutual linking will show that you are a "trusted source."

MEASURING YOUR ONLINE TRAFFIC AND MARKETING RESULTS

What good is optimizing your Web site without knowing how effective your efforts are? It's important that online marketers analyze the results of their efforts and adjust/refine as necessary. Here are the basics on what you should be paying attention to:

- How many people are coming to your site?

- How long are they staying?

- How many folks are repeat visitors?

- Where are they coming from?

- What keywords are they using to find you?

- What are they looking at when they come to your site?

- What is your *bounce rate* (the percentage of users that leave your site without clicking on anything)?

Based on this information, you can more objectively arrange content, work closer with Web sites that are sending you traffic, adjust problems with your homepage that are making people leave without investigating anything, and more. Being able to assess how you are doing online by studying your analytics is a major benefit of online marketing over offline marketing.

The best analytics resource to use when starting out is Google's free analytics program. Although it has fewer bells and whistles than some other programs, it is effective in conveying the basics, and it is incredibly user friendly.

Figure 6.2 is a screenshot of Google's Analytics interface.

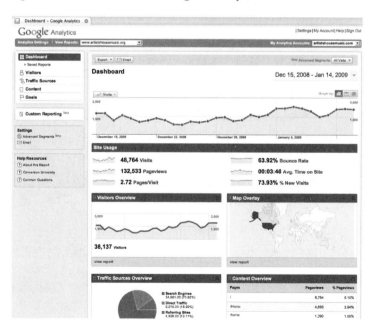

Fig. 6.2. Google Analytics

WHAT IS RSS AND WHY SHOULD I USE IT?

While an effective e-mail list is still incredibly important to keeping your fans up-to-date with your activities, RSS adds a whole new dimension to fan communication.

RSS is an acronym, which stands for **R**eally **S**imple **S**yndication. Basically RSS provides the ability for users to keep on top of updates from dozens of sites without having to actually visit each one. The way it works is like this: a Web site can syndicate its content out as a news "feed," which is automatically sent out to anyone who has signed up to receive this feed. Think of it like an e-mail sign-up, except rather than users getting an e-mail blast from a site with new information, users receive these updates through their RSS reader program. (I happen to use the Google Reader.) The RSS reader compiles all the latest news from sites that the user is interested in and presents all the headlines in one easy-to-navigate page. Users can skim the headlines, or click through to the individual articles and Web sites that they are interested in. It's sort of like a personalized homepage of all the information on the Web. Sites that have an RSS feed will feature an orange icon like this:

Fig. 6.3. RSS Icon

Take a look at the interface of my RSS reader to get an idea of what this looks like:

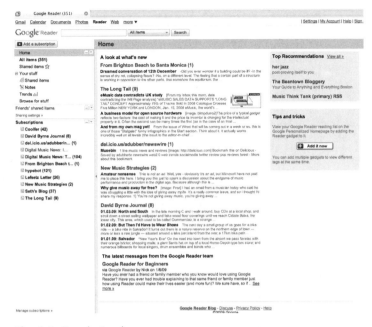

Fig. 6.4. Google Reader

RSS is a great tool for music marketers. First, folks are becoming more and more inundated with e-mail—spam and otherwise. RSS provides an option for people to cut through the information clutter and junk mail, and specify exactly what information that they want to receive. Additionally, content providers (you) don't have to worry about any sort of content management system to send out these updates. It's all automatically done! Users decide what content they want to receive, and it all appears in one centralized place—a "personalized Web site" of all the information they are interested in.

I subscribe to a number of RSS feeds, including one from a great British band called the Clientele, as well as David Byrne's online journal. RSS is also the technology that enables iTunes and other outlets to host Podcasts.

A company called Feedburner (www.feedburner.com, now owned by Google) is a good (and free) way to get started with RSS.

SOCIAL NETWORKING

You are likely aware of the big players currently in the social networking arena: Facebook and MySpace. It makes sense to have a presence on both sites, but there are many other options to consider in terms of using social networks to grow your brand and expand our marketing. The social networking space is changing on a daily basis, and to outline all of the individual players currently out there would be a book upon itself (and one that would constantly need revision!). Instead, here are some broad areas (and some example outlets) that you should be looking at in terms of optimizing your marketing through social networking.

Setting Up Your Own Social Network

Artists are really only limited by their creativity and time when it comes to social network marketing. One option that artists should consider is setting up their own site with all the social networking components already included. It's difficult to build and maintain all the various social networking functions yourself on your own site, which is why a number of artists are using free software (like Ning, www.ning.com) to host chats, and act as an area where fans can update music, images, videos, blogs, and so on. Community members can create their own "page" on the social network (which you as the artist can control) and contribute as much or as little as they want.

Centralizing Your Social Networking Content

There are a number of online artists service-related companies that act as a one-stop shop for updating content on all of your social networking pages. ReverbNation (www.reverbnation.com), out of Durham, NC, is one of the most forward-thinking sites currently available. The site provides users with free, customizable widgets that can be embedded in any social networking site, blog, or other Web site. The widgets can be used to publicize tour dates, play new songs, or announce a new tour, and are all completely trackable! ReverbNation also provides tools for artists to organize online street teams, and provides them with tools that they can use to promote you.

Social Networking "Contest" Sites

Competition brings out the best (or maybe it's the worst?) in all of us. A number of sites are in the business of building online "contest" sites where artists can upload their music, get rated by the communities of the sites, and if they are deemed to be the "best" (over a predetermined period of time), they not only receive recognition on the site, but in many cases, receive a cash prize and/or expert advice and opinion on their song. Two sites are currently leading the pack with this social marketing segment: Famecast and Ourstage. Beyond the financial rewards this exposure can mean, there is a built-in community evaluating your music—a good way to expose your music to new fans!

INSIDER TIP: USING ONLINE MARKETING TO AFFECT OFFLINE RESULTS

It takes a couple of hours for a musician to get started with basic online marketing. Setting up an account with MySpace, Facebook, Twitter, uStream, Flickr, ReverbNation, OurStage, Fanbridge, and the dozens of other options is simple, and an excellent first step. But it's important for artists not to lose sight of the fact that online marketing is not an end on to itself. The most effective online marketing campaigns support the physical marketing efforts as well.

Here are two good examples of artists that are using online means to connect directly with fans to support their offline efforts:

1. JOE PUG

This is from Don Bartlett, manager of Joe Pug, via the Lefsetz letter:

> *"We decided to put an offer up on Joe's Web site and MySpace. We told any fan that if they knew anyone who might be interested in Joe's music, they could send us an e-mail and we would send them as many copies of a two-song sampler CD as they wanted. Free. We even cover the postage. To keep costs down, we invested in a CD publishing system that burns and prints them robotically. Each CD has two songs, contact info, MySpace info, and a reminder that the full CD was at iTunes. If someone lived near a place where a show was scheduled, we printed that show info on there as well. People requested as few as 2 and as many as 50. We sent all of them. Requests continued to pour in, and the more we sent out, the faster the new requests came in. We're at the point now where we get about 15 a day. Joe writes a thank you in each and every one. And almost instantly, sales took off. Show attendance jumped noticeably, and MySpace/Web site action began a steady upward arc. More importantly, we built an incredible database of Joe's most hardcore fans. And after receiving a mailbox full of CDs for free, they are willing to do anything to help forward the cause. And it is the ultimate in target marketing. You have people who already like your music passing it on to their friends, whose tastes they presumably know."*

2. ROCK/JAM BAND UMPHREY'S MCGEE

The band Umphrey's McGee is organizing an online pre-sale campaign that gives their fans a reason to encourage others to buy the record pre-sale. They're announcing it on their Web site, as well as using banner ads on their social networking properties. Here are the details from their site:

> *"Much like an Umphrey's show, no one is exactly sure what will happen with Mantis, the upcoming release from Umphrey's McGee. The more fans that pre-order the release, the more bonus content we'll unlock for everyone. We are leaving the amount of additional content and the makeup of some of that content entirely up to you. There are 8 total levels of material that could be unlocked containing over 45 unique & unreleased audio tracks, including behind-the-scenes perspectives, videos, and plenty of quirky surprises. Bonus Material Part I is available exclusively to those who pre-order."*

THE MOBILE REVOLUTION

Cell Phones and Over-the-Air Downloading

It's taking a while for mobile music technology and OTA (over-the-air) downloads to catch on in the U.S., partly due to users' habits in the U.S., and partly due to unstable and inconsistent technologies and the high pricing models that cell carriers are charging users to download music. As Warner Music Group head Edgar Bronfman Jr. noted, "It's expensive, it's complicated, and it's slow. It's amazing that we've generated as much revenue as we have given how cumbersome the experience can be. So many platforms aren't capable of even the most basic content configurations, like a track bundled with a video."

However, outside of the U.S. (in particular, Asia and Western Europe), the majority of paid downloads are initiated on mobile phones. GReeeeN, a band signed to Universal Music Japan, announced it had sold one million OTA downloads of their single, "Aiuta." Gartner Research, a leading technology research and advisory company, announced in 2007 that consumer spending on mobile music will surpass $32 billion by 2010—despite the fact that carriers must figure out how to develop the right content partnerships, pricing strategies, licensing deals, distribution channels, and marketing, as well as address the host of technical challenges like DRM, storage capacity, and network coverage.

In late 2008, cell phone manufacturer Nokia entered the music business by partnering with all four majors labels to provide their subscribers with unlimited access to the major's catalog. According to Nokia, their "Comes With Music" initiative offers one year of unlimited access to the entire Nokia Music Store catalog, and customers can permanently keep all the music that they have downloaded at the end of the year. The service is not perfect, however, as the tracks are wrapped in Microsoft's PlaysForSure DRM and allow for playback on only one PC and your Nokia cell. It's an interesting step for the labels. It provides them with a new revenue source (a percentage of all phone sales go to them), and is also a way for them to reconnect with music fans who are moving away from traditional CD ownership.

Mobile Marketing

Ringtones

Ringtones are an insanely profitable industry for the major labels, cell carriers, and middleman with revenue of over $5

billion a year worldwide. Currently, the process is decentral-
ized, with different carriers charging different fees for ringtones
that sometimes disappear after ninety days (which is what
Sprint currently does). One would think that it would be easy
to purchase a song from iTunes and convert it to a ringtone
yourself, but the fact is, the labels, cell phone providers, and
middlemen involved in this industry are working hard to keep
the status quo. The copyright laws are both complex and murky,
and involve performance rights, the definition of a "derivative
work," and reproduction rights.

Ringtones for the DIY Musician

Although currently in its infancy, DIY ringtone distribution will
certainly continue to grow as a viable income stream for the independent artist. If you own the copyright of your music, there are
some emerging technologies and companies that make it easy
to edit, create, and sell your own ringtones. New Zealand–based
www.voeveo.com is a ringtone portal that works with independent artists to sell their ringtones online for a 30 percent fee.
(Incidentally, CD Baby currently distributes music to them.)
Another DIY ringtone option is www.MyxerTones.com, which
provides artists with online marketing banners that can be used
to direct traffic from their Web sites or MySpace pages.

Working with a Third Party to Distribute Your Ringtone/Wallpaper

A number of "middleman" technology companies are working to
facilitate the relationship between labels, artists, and cell phone
providers. Gravity Mobile is a third-party technology company
that has relationships with several major cell carriers to provide
ringtones and wallpaper from some great artists and independent labels. The company creates a branded landing page for
each of its partners, which these partners can then use to store
and sell as much content as they want. Indie labels Stones Throw
Records as well as Thrill Jockey currently use the service.

Building Your Community with Mobile Technology

There's been a rise of technology companies that are focused on
enabling artists and labels to effectively expand and communicate with their communities. One example is www.msgme.
com, an easy-to-use keyword-based application that allows
you to communicate information (upcoming shows, new record
information, radio play, etc.) with any fan that chooses to sign
up to hear from you via text messages. Artists set up a keyword
with the service (band name is easiest), market the service to

their existing fan base through their Web site or e-mail list, and upload whatever text message they want their fans to get, whenever they want. Alerts can be pushed out automatically through RSS feeds as well.

An announcement like the following to your e-mail list could be used to get things going:

GET P. JAMES MAGIC SHOW INFO VIA TXT MESG!

That's right, for all you who are usd to wrtng like ths w/out vwls to sv space, P. JAMES MAGIC SHOW now provides show updates via TEXT MESG! It's so easy, it works like this: Send the word "PJAMES" (sans quotes) to 67463. We'll send back info (name, date, details, address, phone) about our next show! Normal text message rates apply with your cell phone carrier.

Universal's Motown imprint launched a text messaging-based marketing initiative with a service similar to msgme called Mozes (www.mozes.com). One of the bands involved in the deal, Hinder, is using the service to offer a live contest each night of their tour, through which fans can text for a chance to win a backstage pass. Fans that opt-in to Hinder's list will be able to text with the band on an ongoing basis and receive exclusive mobile updates.

VIDEO MARKETING

The days are over for labels spending and recouping $7,000,000+ on a music video (which is what Michael Jackson's *Scream* video apparently cost back in 1995—including the $65,000 expense of a computer-generated spaceship).

Traditional video outlets like MTV and VH1 are much more interested in reality TV than promoting new artists. Certain traditional video outlets still make a difference in breaking artists (Country Music Television, for example), but unless you have a marketing budget that is well into six figures, it's not realistic to expect that you can effectively compete with the Faith Hills and Vince Gills of the world.

The rise in online music video outlets, such as YouTube and inexpensive video editing software, have enabled independent (and major label) artists and labels to create effective videos and widely distribute them for a fraction of the cost of creating and promoting a "professional" video.

Viral Videos Can't Be Manufactured, but...

There is no surefire way to make a video viral. However, there are some guidelines that you can use to make the most of the video format as a promotional tool, and with some luck, a viral sensation.

One of my favorite labels, Stones Throw Records, puts out records from an extremely prolific artist called Madlib. To announce the release of Madlib's *Beat Konducta in India* record, the label created a wonderful (and inexpensive!) video promo that showcased Madlib's new music being played over vintage Rajini (a south Indian actor affectionately known as "Superstar") films. Stones Throw Records accomplished a couple of things with this video promo:

1. By incorporating cuts from Rajini films into this promo, Stones Throw is creating a great point of reference for the release. I know exactly what to expect when I get the record.

2. The video incorporates samples from the new record, and continues to build my interest in the record.

3. It's incredibly creative and makes me want to send it to my friends.

4. It's funny, which also makes me want to send it to my friends.

5. It is effective in its main function as a prerelease video: the CD release date is announced several times within the video.

I may already be a fan of Madlib and the Stones Throw Records label, but this video makes me want to share it with folks that can potentially become new fans. This is a huge part of the mechanism that qualifies this video as "viral."

Other Ways to Raise the Visibility of Your Band or Label through Video

Third-Party Visibility. Creating a dedicated channel on YouTube or any of the various online video sites is an obvious way to get your content out. Fans would visit your channel to see a variety of videos of your band, perhaps interviews with band members, snippets of live performance, etc. Many of these sites have built-in mechanisms to help you grow your community: fans can subscribe to your channel, share your videos with friends, and share their opinions through comments and forums (like those on Imeem.com). Covering a popular song on YouTube is a good way to get new people interested in your band, too.

Offering live A/V broadcasts (from your home studio or anywhere else) is another outstanding way to connect with fans. Companies such as www.Ustream.tv (popularized by 50 Cent!), Mogulus, and Stickam offer free software that makes creating live video chats, or previewing your new songs live and in person to loyal fans, easier than ever.

There are also online tools available that artists can use to easily distribute video content to multiple video sites at once. Tube-Mogul (www.tubemogul.com) is an online video distributor that can automatically deliver your video content to various sites (currently twenty video sites are on board), and also provide you with in-depth analytics on the number of folks that are watching your videos.

Your Own Site Visibility. It's easier than ever to have video content on your own site, too. If you don't have the bandwidth or tech savvy to host your videos on your own, YouTube, MySpace, Imeem, and others provide a code that you can use to imbed the videos you've posted on these sites onto your own site. Make these embed codes public on your own site so folks can use them on their blogs and Web sites.

Personalize your content. Post live videos, videos of you in the studio, interviews, in-store performances—anything that can help to personalize you and your music.

Contests: iMovie and other editing software programs are inexpensive, easy to use, and common. It's likely that a percentage of your fan base is using them. A "Make Our Video" contest is a great way to get your fans involved in your promotion.

INSIDER TIP: PRETTY GIRLS MAKE GRAVES "MAKE OUR VIDEO" CONTEST

Matador records worked with YouTube for the indie band Pretty Girls Make Graves "Make Our Video" contest. Matador promoted the contest on the PGMG MySpace page, on www.matador.com, and in the label's newsletter blasts. They also worked with YouTube to get the contest homepage visibility on its site. Dubbed the "first-ever music video contest on YouTube," the contest served several purposes. It was a great way to raise visibility for the band and promote an upcoming record release date. Secondly, it promoted the label's other current releases, which were offered as prizes. And finally, it was a great way to mobilize the video-savvy fans of PGMG and have them spread their own video creations for the band. This is a great way to start a viral video campaign. Original copy for the contest is below:

Welcome to the official YouTube group for the Pretty Girls Make Graves "Make Our Video" contest, where you can win the first-ever music video contest on YouTube for a band who has toured the world with Bloc Party, Franz Ferdinand, and Death Cab for Cutie.

In addition to adding the title "music video maker" to your résumé, the winner will be given $1,000 in cold, hard cash and be flown out to New York all-expenses-paid to hang with the band and see them live in concert courtesy of Matador records. You'll receive spending cash and your flight, your hotel, even your food will be paid for in this exclusive contest.

For the 20 runner-ups, you'll get a Matador Records prize pack, including signed CDs, posters, and a bunch of music from artists like Mogwai, Cat Power, Mission of Burma, Belle and Sebastian, Early Man, Pavement, Interpol, and the New Pornographers.

You can also listen to songs from Pretty Girls Make Graves' upcoming album **Elan Vital** *on the band's MySpace profile located at:*

http://www.myspace.com/prettygirlsmakegraves

Expectations

A lot of folks remember Nirvana breaking onto the scene with their *Smells Like Teen Spirit* video in 1991. This video definitely had a lot to do with *Nevermind* selling more than 10 million copies since its release, but the music industry is now a completely different animal. In the past, videos in heavy rotation on MTV meant a tangible increase in record sales. These days, instead of making a huge impact on sales, videos make an impact on other things: touring, recognition, community building, and appearances—the things that now are a more reliable income generator than record sales.

Summary

Online marketing is a rapidly growing (and evolving) segment of music marketing. The players involved in the segment may change over time, but the principles of online marketing for developing musicians will not: use the available online tools wisely to attract and convert folks into fans of your music, then provide your community with effective tools to communicate their interest in your music to as many people as possible.

While the concepts and skills we talked about in this chapter provide for a great background, it's imperative that you stay on top of emerging technologies and new business models, particularly in the mobile marketing space!

Workshop

- What specific techniques are you going to use to make your site unique, interactive, and a place that people will want to come back to?

- What ideas for viral content do you have? How will you present these on your site?

- Using the free keyword resource tool on Wordtracker, create a keyword strategy for your site. What words will you use in the Title, Description, and Keyword fields in your metadata?

- What kind of contests/incentives do you think would be effective using online, mobile, or video marketing?

TWO

Advertising Considerations, Marketing to Press and Radio, and Making the Most of Your National Tour

7 Advertising

Prior to becoming one of the most highly regarded guitar players and composers of the twentieth century, Frank Zappa worked for a period of time in the advertising business. Frank used this experience to help guide his early ad campaigns for the Verve label. In a 1988 interview with Bob Marshall, Frank had the following to say about advertising:

> *I wish there was a way to graph this out, but advertising is very powerful, and in order for advertising to work, it works on a nonlogical, subconscious, psychological level. And to induce people to buy things they don't need, for reasons which are not there, they have to trick you. And they trick you with colors; they trick you with modifying the cutting rate of the commercial, which then modifies the way in which you ingest the data. They do tricks, and part of what's involved in the data that they are tricking you into consuming is this built-in dread factor: "You can fail. Someone will laugh at you. You are impotent. You will be poor. You will die!" Various flavors of dread, they're lurking in there in different combinations, and, of course, after they've shown you the dread, they show you the light at the end of the tunnel: "Our product will allow you not to die. You will not have pain. These little yellow pills, this really works. Our car goes fast and it's red." That's all built in there, okay. So, people have been conditioned to consuming the dread factor. They don't know they're getting the dread, but it's in there. And then the answer to their problems—a product. So, they're trading dollars to avoid the dread, and the dollars will be aimed in the direction of the product that solves this imaginary problem.*

The tactics Frank talks about here are perhaps employed more by people that put together late-night infomercials than folks that put together ads that market music, but the end result still holds true for any kind of advertising: your product (your band/ your music) needs to create an emotional connection with the listener.

PRINT ADVERTISING OPTIONS: CONSUMER, TRADE, AND CO-OP PRINT ADS

Advertising is a way to make an additional impression on someone that may have heard your music on the radio, read about you online or offline, saw your name in the show listing in the local weekly, and so on. While advertising does not necessarily "lead the charge" in any music marketing campaign, it is still an important element. Frank Zappa was right when he said that it exists on a subconscious and psychological level. It serves as a way to bring your band or your music to the forefront of someone's mind, and it can function as the "tipping point" that all records need in order to appeal to the larger population.

In terms of advertising, print advertising is about as old school as you get. But until *Rolling Stone's* circulation drops from 1.3 million to 0 and all magazines are delivered online, print advertising will continue to be a valid and effective way to reach potential customers.

Here are the outlets that music marketers are working with in the print world.

Consumer Advertising

As the name suggests, consumer advertising consists of placements designed to positively affect music consumers. From *Rolling Stone* on down to fanzines (or 'zines, which are most commonly small-circulation, specialized publications) like *Signal To Noise* or *The Big Takeover*, consumer print ads constitute the bulk of most record release advertising.

INSIDER TIP: EXAMPLES OF CONSUMER PRINT ADS

Music Release Ads in *Paste* magazine.

Fig. 7.1. Full Page Label Ad. For Rounder Records (with a rather clichéd title!).

Fig. 7.2. Half Page Ad. Announces Of Montreal's new record.

Fig. 7.3. Sixth Fractional Strip Ad. For a covers record by Jesse Malin.

Trade Advertising

Trade publications are designed to affect the music industry itself, rather than consumers. *Billboard, Radio and Records*, and *CMJ* are some of the top examples. Particularly with the radio-focused trade outlets, marketers that take out ads in these trade outlets want to build a buzz on an artist with the hopes that other industry folks will want to be a part of this amazing event. Radio trade ads typically call out the single that the label is working, and point out the fact that the record is "Ready to Chart!" and "Breaking" at popular stations around the country.

Co-Op Print Advertising

Co-op advertising is advertising that is paid by labels to retailers. Sometimes it is used for visibility in the store, but retailers will also advertise new releases or catalog sales in local weeklies, usually with just a *mini* (industry speak for a thumbnail image of the record cover), title, and sale price, along with several other releases. Retailers will typically place dedicated ads promoting a single release if that artist is (a) a major artist and has provided an added value item to the retailer, like a CD sampler, or (b) an artist that is performing live in the store. Again, the label, not the retailer, pays for these ads.

RESEARCHING YOUR PRINT ADVERTISING OUTLETS

Print ads can be expensive. The current rate card price for a fractional quarter-page color ad in *Rolling Stone* is over $40,000, with a full page going for over $145,000. Even with relatively smaller "tastemakers" like *Magnet* magazine, you are likely going to pay at least $1,000 per insertion for a 4/C (full color) ad in a magazine with national distribution. So before you think about plunking down your hard-earned cash for a print ad, it's important that you research your options extensively to find the vehicle that is the perfect fit for you.

Here are the main considerations:

- Identify what publications your target audience reads.
- Determine which of those publications best suit you, your budget, and what you are trying to accomplish.

As an example, if your band has a Wilco feel to it, you're likely going to want to get coverage in a songwriter-based magazine like *American Songwriter* or *Performing Songwriter*. While the editorial coverage in each of these magazines needs to be considered, there are a number of basic questions that you need to ask the ad rep to be sure you are making the most appropriate choice.

Before booking an ad, always determine the following with your potential advertising outlet.

What is your magazine's demographic?

This should be question number 1. If you're in a grind-core band, you're probably looking to advertise in a magazine whose readers are younger and primarily male. Remember to look beyond just music publications, but also look at other magazines they may read, such as skating, surfing, and other publications.

How many subscribers do you have?

A magazine's number of subscribers (the people that pay to have the publication delivered to them directly) is key. Advertisers always flaunt their circulation numbers, which are much less important than the number of subscribers they have. Circulation refers to the number of magazines or newspapers that the publisher prints, which includes not just subscribers but also the free stacks that they drop off at kiosks, lobbies, etc.—and no one knows if all of those publications are read. For example, I get dozens (as do other marketing folks at Berklee) of magazines every couple of weeks from ad sales reps that want me to advertise with their publication. Most of these simply do not get read (Recycled? Yes. Read? No...), yet the magazines include these free issues, as well as the thousands of other free issues they send out to similar ad buyers, in their circulation numbers. As a result, circulation numbers are not necessarily accurate representations of the amount of people that actually read the magazine. Subscription numbers are not always posted in the magazine's media kit, especially if the number is low—but subscription numbers are a much more accurate way to determine the actual readership of the magazine.

INSIDER TIP: PASS THROUGH

If the ad rep starts talking about a "pass through" or "pass along" number (which is basically the idea that a magazine is left somewhere and someone else will read it), you should realize that this is a completely made up number, and no credence should be given to it at all.

Where is your magazine distributed?

Your major concern should be the magazine's subscribers. But in the case of targeted fanzines, especially the free ones with low subscription rates, it's important to know exactly where your ad will be appearing. For example, there's a great fanzine called *Arthur* that distributes a number of issues directly to some amazing music events in the indie rock world, in addition to hip record stores, coffee shops, and other artsy outlets. If this is your audience, then advertising in this publication might make sense for you.

How much money do your readers spend on music?

This is less of a concern than any of the above questions, as it is more or less a given that if you advertise in a music magazine, the readers do purchase music. However, if for some reason you have the idea to advertise in *Outdoor Life* or *Hot Rod* magazine, it makes sense to find out if their readers even think about purchasing music. Ad reps will likely have this information, or something similar, at the ready.

Having answers to all of these above questions will help you get a better indication of not only the readership of the publication, but will also affect how you tailor your ad to them.

INSIDER TIP: TAILORING YOUR AD

Tailoring your ad is an important part of an artist's advertising strategy. The same copy and images that work for a singer-songwriter in *Performing Songwriter* might not be as effective in *Utne Reader*, for example. It makes sense to stay as consistent as you can to reinforce your message, but do be aware of small adjustments (like a quote, for example) that might be more effective if changed from one outlet to another.

MEDIA ADVERTISING: RADIO AND TELEVISION

The same principles and essential questions that pertain to print advertising hold true for radio and TV advertising. Although it's on a grander level and the production elements are different, you are still trying to reach a particular demographic, and need to know the same things from these media outlets as print media outlets.

Unlike print advertising, where the costs you pay to advertise are determined by the size of your ad, with television and radio, the prices are determined by market and listeners. To use a very obvious example, the pinnacle of television advertising would be ads run during the Super Bowl where the market is "almost everyone" and the viewers are also "almost everyone." As a result, they are very expensive. Commercials during less popular shows are considerably less expensive than the $2.4 million it costs for a Super Bowl ad, but are still in the $100,000 range for national visibility.

The standard half hour of television contains 22 minutes of program and 8 minutes of commercials, which is broken down into 6 minutes of national ads and 2 minutes of local. A 30-second time slot in a medium market can be purchased for (relatively) cheap—as little as $5 per 1,000 viewers.

Radio operates in a similar manner, but much cheaper. Advertisers are able to pick and choose national vs. regional outlets, particular shows they want to support, and the time they want their ads to run. The most expensive ads are those during rush-hour drive time.

Keep in mind: TV and radio ads are a very expensive advertising choice. In addition to the cost of booking the ads, there are steep production costs associated with TV ads. Additionally, the results for artists that are not semi-superstar are often negligible.

INSIDER TIP: RESPONDING TO SALES SPIKES

When the National Public Radio (NPR) piece on Ryko's *Voices on the Verge* hit, sales immediately shot through the roof. The increased sales and attention made us adjust our marketing plan accordingly. We booked some radio spots in our target markets during the exact time that the NPR piece ran (evening drive time), thinking that it might appeal to the same demographic in different cities. It seemed like a good idea. However, we saw no spike in sales from the ads in these markets. In hindsight, the money may have been better spent at retail or on additional press support.

ONLINE ADVERTISING

Online advertising can be a great complement to your press, touring, and sales efforts, and very useful in building your general visibility in the increasingly important online music world.

Online advertising is one of the most popular and fastest growing forms of advertising today. As more and more fans go online to get their music-related (and nonmusic related!) news, the more effective and pricy online advertising becomes. Let's discuss some of the more popular online advertising methods in use today by music marketers:

Banner Ads

Banner ads consist of small pieces of real estate on a Web site (measured in terms of pixels rather than inches or centimeters) that provide advertisers with the ability to post artwork and a link to a third-party site of their choosing—typically their own Web site. Banner ads are typically created by the same designer that you use to handle the rest of your advertising materials, and are either static (they show one image only) or rotating (several images can be displayed).

Benefits of Online Advertising through Banner Ads

- You can direct folks to wherever you want them to go on your Web site: sales page, tour page, or a contest page. It's potentially a much more active form of advertising than a print ad.

- It offers many more options for creative art than a print ad.

- Banner ads can be updated quickly and easily to represent positive press quotes or updated tour dates.

- Banner ads are generally less expensive than print ads for the same number of impressions.

Downside

- Folks tend to ignore banner ads even more than print ads! (It's a big downside!)

How It Works

The same level of research that you put into determining where you advertise for print should be applied to your online campaign. A potential site's demographic, level of editorial, and online reach (how many visitors turn up daily to the site) are all important to consider. Web advertising rates vary widely—and they're often negotiable—but Web sites generally charge for advertisers in one of two ways:

Per Impression (CPM)

This is the most common form of online pricing that you will find. Sites that collect advertising revenue on a per-impression (the amount of times an ad is viewed) basis charge advertisers based on the amount of times they serve the ad on their site. For example, Pitchforkmedia.com, a wildly popular "tastemaker" site generally covering independent artists, currently charges $3.50 to $8.00 per thousand impressions (CPM = cost per thousand), with minimum buys of 100,000 to 300,000 impressions, depending on the size of the ad. In order for a medium-sized ad to appear 250,000 times on Pitchfork, for example, an advertiser would spend $1,250. With impression-based pricing rates, there is no guarantee that anyone will click your ad.

Price Per Click (PPC)

This online advertising model is more popular as a way to purchase keywords with the search engines, but some music-focused sites work on a PPC (**P**rice **P**er **C**lick) model. With this model, the advertiser guarantees a certain amount of clicks, rather than a certain amount of served impressions. PPC is the best choice for advertisers, if you can get it!

INSIDER TIP: NEGOTIATING AD RATES

Negotiating with ad reps is a process not unlike negotiating with vendors at Istanbul's Grand Bazaar. First, *never* pay rate card prices for online or print ads! Ad rates are highly negotiable, and ad reps expect that there will be some give and take involved. Second, if you are going to be paying for advertising, always enquire about any value-adds that you can get to go along with your ad. With the print magazine industry in a state of flux, advertisers are more willing to provide additional exposure (such as a Web banner ad, or a mention in their newsletter) to those who purchase print advertising.

Newsletter Visibility

Another online advertising avenue for marketers is visibility in third-party newsletters. Blogs, tastemakers, and online/physical retailers often create regular editorial-based newsletters to which marketers can either contribute banner ads or short editorial copy. These outlets offer a great advertising vehicle for folks to reach a highly targeted music base.

Keyword Buys

A third form of online advertising is of the search engine variety. I'm only bringing this up to round out the online advertising outlets available; it really makes little financial sense at this point for a band or label to purchase keywords online to increase their visibility. Basically, Google, Yahoo, MSN, and other search engines provide the option for advertisers to purchase keywords on a CPC basis. The process is done through an online auction, with the highest bidder getting the prime positioning. Advertisers are allowed to provide short descriptive copy and a link to their site. They provide a budget (daily, weekly, monthly, etc.) that is decreased with every click that the search engine provides. Again, this is not a real viable option for bands and labels. If your site is well optimized (as we discussed in the online marketing chapter), you will appear at the top of the search returns anyway.

COMPONENTS OF AN EFFECTIVE AD

Ads (both online and print) need to catch the attention of the viewer and convey your message in the shortest amount of time possible.

Although ads are placed for a variety of reasons by labels and artists (label branding ads, artist tour ads, record release ads, congratulatory trade ads, and so on), ads are primarily composed of the following elements:

Headline

David Ogilvy, considered the father of modern advertising, understood the power of an effective headline. One of the most famous headlines attributed to Ogilvy was for his client Rolls Royce: "At 60 miles an hour, the loudest noise in this new Rolls Royce comes from the electric clock." While it's debatable whether or not Ogilvy actually personally wrote the headline or "co-opted" it from a review of the vehicle, the point is that he encapsulated luxury, superiority, personality, durability, and a positive brand experience in less than twenty words. Anyone who sees this ad immediately knows what Rolls Royce is all about. Ogilvy created that headline more than fifty years ago, but the same core tenets he used hold true for advertising today.

The headlines of most music ads you see announcing new releases are going to be the name of the artist and the title of the new record. This is fine, and every impression you can make on someone is great. However, the best headlines are those that work to engage the viewer a bit more through humor, amazing press quotes, creative thinking, or as with Ogilvy, conveying a message in as few words as possible.

I worked on a couple of Bill Hicks records at Ryko, and we created an ad campaign based on the legendary *Everyone Digs Bill Evans* record cover. We created a headline in a similar font to the Evans record, *Everybody Digs Bill Hicks*. We secured quotes from Gruff Rhys (leader of Super Furry Animals; he provided quotes both in Welsh and English!), from David Cross, Maynard Keenan (from Tool), Radiohead, and others. Tom Waits gave us the quote, "Bill Hicks—blowtorch, excavator, truthsayer, and brain specialist, like a reverend waving a gun around. He will correct your vision. Others will drive on the road he built.

Long may his records rant even though he can't." We worked out an advertising campaign that we thought might be a bit more engaging than simply listing his name and his records large up top.

Quotes are also effective as headlines. If *The New York Times* has called you "the next Bob Dylan" in a review, this quote needs to be up top, HUGE. And remember, your graphic designer is your best friend when it comes to working out ad campaigns. Run through some ideas, and see if the two of you can tie in the creative with the headline and the overall ad concept.

Description/Press Quotes

Beneath the headline, music ads typically provide a description of what's interesting about your record, or a listing of tour dates if that's what you want folks to come away with. The amount of descriptive copy is usually dictated by how familiar you think people are with the artist. Emerging artists will likely need to add some additional copy to bring folks up to speed with the sound, and perhaps list some points of reference. For example, "Soul classics in the style of Al Green and Marvin Gaye..." or "From the school of Grant Green and Wes Montgomery." For artists that are more familiar, less copy is probably the way to go. If Prince is putting out a new record, there's really no need to explain what it's going to sound like, unless he's putting out a stripped down acoustic record, which would be very different than previous releases. Additionally, wherever possible, use press quotes as your descriptors rather than your own copy.

Call to Action

The final thing you need to lay out on your ad is the "action" you want the reader to take after viewing your ad. What do you want your reader to do after checking out your ad? Are you running a contest on your Web site for fans to get free backstage passes? Are you offering a free download of the first single off your record? Do you simply want folks to know that your record comes out in three weeks? With banner ads, it's a bit easier to come up with a call to action; people can simply click and go to the page you want them to go to. With print ads, it's important that you indicate the call to action as clearly and succinctly as possible. A large and in-charge call to action is the best course of action:

Live at the Abbey Lounge
Available In Stores and Online July 17!
Buy NOW at: www.PJamesMagicShow.com

Additional Things to Consider

- Tagging a specific retailer (like Amazon, CIMS, Barnes & Noble, etc.) by adding their logo to the bottom of your ads will help to increase their buy-in of your record.

- Measure twice and cut once: Triple-check your ad before you deliver it to the publication. There's nothing worse than seeing an ad you've submitted with a silly grammatical mistake.

- Make sure it is the proper file format! Magazines employ production people whose job it is to be sure your ad is print quality, but everyone makes mistakes. Be sure you don't make one by submitting an incorrect file or a low-res version.

INSIDER TIP: LESS IS MORE

Mark Sandman from the guitar-less "low rock" trio Morphine used to say that making music was like making tomato sauce: less is more. It's a good way to make music, and it's a good way to lay out copy for ads. Try to avoid the temptation of cramming as much descriptive copy into your ads as possible. You'll end up with a dense mess that no one will read. Quick bullet points, striking headlines, and concise calls to action are the ingredients to an effective ad.

TIMING YOUR AD CAMPAIGN

Most music ad campaigns are booked to support a new release, and perhaps a tour surrounding the release. We'll talk more about the specific timing of tour support advertising later on, but for a new release ad campaign, it makes sense to begin thinking about what outlets to advertise in twelve weeks out from the release date, at about the same point you're thinking about press, radio, and retail opportunities. Turnaround time with banner ads is very quick, as there is next to no production time involved, but some national consumer magazines work many months in advance. Space reservations are sometimes booked two months in advance, and art is generally due six to eight weeks prior to street date. As with most things, planning ahead saves frustration (and money) later on.

Ads that support specific releases are generally booked to run the month prior to, and possibly the month of, the release of the record. The idea is that press, radio, and retail visibility are generally at their height just prior to and during the month of the record release. As we discussed, advertising does not lead your marketing campaign; its job is to complement other forms of marketing already happening. If you find that your record "has legs" (is still on the upswing with sales and buzz several months out from release), you can always place a phase-2 ad campaign as well.

Summary

There are a number of advertising options available to musicians: print, online, television, and radio. We looked at what questions to ask potential advertising outlets, how to determine what advertising vehicle is the best choice for you, how online advertising differs from print advertising, the components that make up an effective ad, and when you should be timing and placing your ad. I hope you've found that advertising is a relatively straightforward part of the marketing palette. While it may take a while to perfect your ad and your message, the fundamentals are easy to understand and implement: find out where your fans are, and deliver a concise, action-driven message to them.

Workshop

Assume you are advertising a new release that hits the streets on September 12th, and have a budget of $10,000 to work with. Create an advertising plan that addresses the following:

- The media outlet you would like to advertise in
- The size of the ad
- The frequency of your ad (for nonprint ads)
- The cost of the ad
- The issue street date (or date that the online/radio/TV ad hits) for each outlet
- The creative due date for each outlet
- The size specifications of your ad (e.g., 7.5" x 10" if this is a print ad)
- The delivery instructions for each
- If the ad will be color or black and white
- Once you have your plan together, consider the following:
- Why did you choose these outlets?
- How did you determine what size ads to run?

- What are the current circulation and subscription numbers for these outlets? (If you are including radio, television, or online outlets, please list appropriate viewers/listenership/ site traffic.)

- Assuming your record's street date is September 12th, which issue street date is most appropriate for you?

8 Publicity

Outside of online marketing, one of the only other relatively level playing fields for independent artists is publicity. In terms of music, publicity can be defined as targeting and connecting with people in the media (writers for print publications or online outlets, television talent bookers, and in some cases radio personalities) with the end goal of persuading these "tastemakers" to provide you with some degree of visibility. Press outlets are still a very important piece of the overall marketing puzzle, and positive reviews in some of the more popular national or regional outlets can not only have a tangible effect on sales, but they can also help to energize show attendance and convince others in the industry that your music is worth listening to.

It's entirely possible for unsigned artists to get the same media coverage as major label artists based largely on the merits of their record, live show, and the intangible "buzz" that occurs when artists begin to reach the tipping point. Having said that, one important point: while it is possible to get similar coverage as major labels, it is not easy. Let's discuss what the writers are looking for from you and how you can present your music and story to them in the best possible light.

PRESS KIT ESSENTIALS

The music industry tends to be a jaded group to start with, and nothing raises the ire of these folks more than a poorly planned and executed press kit. A poor press kit is sure to keep music un-listened to, and the rest of your kit is sure to be sent to the circular bin "with a bullet," as they say. The good news is that the elements that make up an effective press kit are straightforward, and the essentials are not going to change much from band to band.

The goal of the promo kit is to have the kit itself forgotten.

When putting together your press kit, the first rule of thumb is to put yourself in the shoes of the people who receive these things on a daily basis. The music writers at the major locals like *The Boston Globe* and *The Chicago Tribune* receive dozens of press kits a day, and the fact is, the fewer barriers (extraneous material) you put between them and your story/music, the greater chance there is of them listening. While you may have the urge to create something that really stands out from the crowd, the bells and whistles may in fact get in the way. I urge you to reconsider and instead let your music, bio, and press clippings do the talking for you. Like many things in life, simple really is better.

So What Makes a Good Press Kit?

An effective press kit contains the following:

- bio/press release
- an advance or finished product
- link to hi-res photos
- press quotes (this could also be part of the bio/press release)

Press Release/Bio

A *press release/bio* is simply a one-sheet document (perhaps double sided, if you have a lot of important information) outlining the background of the band, and the specifics of the record you are promoting. The press release provides writers with the background they need to help form their story, and should also get them excited about wanting to actually hear your music. We'll get into more detail on presenting a story to press, but the main point of your press release and bio should be to set the stage: identify what makes you unique, highlight individual background/accomplishments of the members if they are interesting, point out any career highlights so far, provide information on tour dates, and perhaps share some key press quotes. You'll find that many writers, especially the daily and weekly writers, copy and paste directly out of your press release and bio. So make it good. And don't forget to add the street date!

Your Advance or Finished Product

Currently, writers still like to be serviced with a physical piece (especially for new artists). If you are making advances for press, be sure your (or your publicist's) contact info is all over it. CDs easily get separated from their boxes in a pile of to-review music. If you are sending out finished product, be sure that you are sending out a full art version.

Photo

Photos sometimes make the difference between whether something will run or not. Hi-res press photos are a necessity. Back in the day, press releases routinely contained a glossy shot, but these days, the norm is to provide a link to your Web site where a writer could download a 300 dpi hi-res image. Writers sometimes finish their articles at 2 a.m. the night before deadline. If there is a private link for media to hi-res shots, it ensures that the photos will run!

Press Quotes/Clippings

If you've had some past success with the press, your promo kit should include a "paste-up" of this media coverage. Format is important here. Any editorial your band gets should be cut out from whatever else surrounds it in the paper. Cut out the masthead of the publication, affix it on a piece of paper with the article below, and be sure to format it all so it looks nice on an 8 ½" x 11" piece of paper. Alternatively, if you have some really key quotes, these can simply be dropped into your press release or bio.

Optional Materials

Cover Letter

It's definitely not necessary, and odds are it won't be read, but a very quick introduction, a note of thanks, some key bullet points on the project, and your contact info in a cover letter might please a writer here or there. Again, if you are working with a publicist, this is less necessary because the writer likely has a relationship with the publicist, will hear from them on the phone, and an intro is not necessary.

Tour Itinerary

If you have a busy tour schedule, include an itinerary of upcoming shows as well. If the recipient of your kit is not all that familiar with your band and they see you're playing places like the 9:30 Club in D.C. or Yoshi's in San Francisco, they'll know you are the real deal. This is particularly important for show preview or review press.

PRESS RELEASE FOR CHUCK E. WEISS: *OLD SOULS & WOLF TICKETS*

Release date: January 22, 2002

CHUCK E. WEISS: Old Souls & Wolf Tickets

"I don't know why I gravitated towards it like I did. I think it was my father. He used to turn on this station when I was a kid that played a lot of swing and boogie woogie, and I used to flip out. Before I could talk, I was listening to this stuff."

—Chuck E. Weiss on boogie-woogie and the damage done, October 2001

On his second Rykodisc/Slow River album, *Old Souls & Wolf Tickets*, L.A.'s mythic mystical returns from a three-year absence with perhaps the finest record of his enigmatic career. Featuring thirteen original compositions and a recently unearthed 1970 duet with blues legend Willie Dixon, *Old Souls* may very well be Chuck E. Weiss' defining moment. Taking up where his acclaimed 1999 album *Extremely Cool* left off, *Old Souls & Wolf Tickets* finds Chuck E. and his accomplices trafficking hard musical goods—potent barfly blues, tiki club jazz, lunatic jive, and weird, incantational R&B.

Weiss' lordly reputation among the hipster cognoscenti is well documented, but here he outdoes himself. On tracks such as "It Don't Happen Overnight," "Anthem for Old Souls," and "Sweetie-O," he emerges as a ruthless emotional manipulator, inducing tears one minute, gut-splitting hilarity the next.

The new collection once and for all cements Weiss' reputation as America's unsung King of Jive. As on his previous album, Weiss is again abetted by his longtime band the G-d Damn Liars, a motley assortment of roots-rock icons, including guitarist Tony Gilkyson, Spyder Mittelman on sax, bassists Will McGregor and Steve Nelson, drummers Jim Christie and Don Heffington, and pianists John Herron and Mike Murphy. But where *Extremely Cool* was a paean to Weiss' adopted L.A. hometown, *Old Souls & Wolf Tickets* is largely inspired by a different place and time.

"I reverted back further to when I was a kid growing up in Denver," Weiss explains. "Like the song 'Sneaky Jesus.' All the people I mention there are real bizarre characters I grew up with. 'Blood Alley' is about this place across from my junior high. There would be gang fights every evening after school let out. About 3:20 every school day, you knew there'd be a rumble."

Though the new album chronicles some of Weiss' fondest Colorado memories, *Old Souls & Wolf Tickets* is ultimately a musical tour of America, with a few cosmic layovers in between. The singer imagines going out New Orleans style on "Dixieland Funeral," while "Congo Square at Midnight" celebrates those rambunctious Louisiana days before Louis Armstrong and Storyville. "Jolie's Nightmare" is Chuck E.'s fractured homage to Al Jolson, the pioneering vaudevillian whose Eurocentric take on African-American performing presaged Elvis Presley.

Recalls Chuck E.: "I always thought of Al Jolson as a ham, but he was absolutely worshipped by every Jewish family. My dad used to speak of him in the same tone as he spoke of God..."

"Ain't ya got ears son? That little Jew boy with the big old head be one of the best musicians in this town, this country even."

– Willie Dixon on Chuck E. Weiss, circa the late 1980s.

Its original compositions notwithstanding, *Old Souls & Wolf Tickets'* most curious track is a cover tune recorded more than thirty years ago in Boulder, Colorado. "Down the Road a Piece" features Chuck E. and bassist-singer Willie Dixon fronting the Chicago All-Stars, a blues supergroup featuring pianist Sunnyland Slim, guitarist Buster Benton, drummer Clifford James, and harmonica legend Carey Bell.

Chuck E. recalls how the All-Stars booked time at Boulder's low-tech Bananaland Studios to capture the big-room vibe of classic blues recordings. He also remembers how his youthful enthusiasm nearly sabotaged the 1970 sessions.

"They wanted me to kind of settle down," he recalls with a laugh. "I was too anxious. I was like, 'Come on, let's go!' You know how teenagers are. Willie and the guys just said, 'Settle down, you'll be all right.' Listening to it now, it's kind of cute hearing a younger version of myself."

> *"Chuck E.'s always been a purist—not of this world, if ya know what I mean. Got this vision and won't let reality stand in its way."*

> *– Tom Waits on Chuck E. Weiss, 1998*

> *"Nobody told you it would be easy, 'cause it don't happen overnight..."*

> *"It Don't Happen Overnight" by Chuck E. Weiss, 2001*

Though *Old Souls & Wolf Tickets* possesses the footloose feel of a one-take session it is, in fact, the culmination of a strange, lifelong journey. The son of an inventor, Weiss was still in his teens when he wangled a gig pounding the skins for blues legend Lightnin' Hopkins. In the years that followed, he found himself jamming, touring and/or recording with the luminous likes of Willie Dixon, Dr. John, Tom Waits, Roger Miller, and Spencer Davis. He's got the pictures to prove it. The tapes, too.

Weiss' résumé would be impressive enough had he simply performed with some of the world's most respected blues idols and folk heroes. But the other piece of the Chuck E. saga has to do with his Svengali-like influence on L.A.'s hipster-folk music scene. During the late seventies, Chuck E. lived at the Tropicana Motel, the same West Hollywood dive where Tom Waits and Rickie Lee Jones hung their porkpie hats. It was around this time that Weiss began demonstrating a con artist's penchant for outlandish storytelling. To this day, one does not know if Chuck E.'s on the level when he says his Aunt Lottie was an ex-Ziegfeld Girl with connections to Fanny Brice (interestingly enough, "passing out wolf tickets" is forties slang for stirring up trouble). Perhaps it was this gift for the put-on that inspired Jones to immortalize Weiss in her Top 5 hit, "Chuck E.'s In Love."

In 1981, Chuck E. signed with Select Records and released an album of rough-hewn demo tapes titled *The Other Side Of Town*. Then, with his professional future looking brighter than ever, Chuck E. disappeared from the international recording fold like so much evaporating smoke. Years later, he would explain his sudden disappearance thusly: "I was distracted."

> *"If you dig twisted jungle music, sinful, quick dirty sex, and the old boogie, listen up."*

> *—Eddy Little on Chuck E's "comeback" album,* Extremely Cool, *circa 1999*

After an 18-year recording hiatus, Chuck E. unexpectedly resurfaced in 1999 with the astounding *Extremely Cool*. Critical acclaim was immediate and unequivocal. *Rolling Stone* called the disc "an anthology of hipster tastes—jazz, spoken word, blues, Cajun, New Orleans R&B," while *Billboard* hailed it as "...a return to form for a long-lost underground icon." *Pulse!* made favorable comparisons to R&B legends like Louis Jordan, Tiny Bradshaw, Son House, Cootie Williams, and Lord Buckley. Entertainment Weekly called the disc "...perhaps the weirdest good album you'll spin this year."

It would be an understatement to say Chuck E. was surprised by the warm critical and retail reception. "I was flabbergasted," he says. "I thought it would do okay, but I didn't think it was gonna do great. I didn't think I would get the kind of reviews I got. I was really pleased."

Now, with the release of his new album, Chuck E. Weiss continues the musical journey he started years ago in Denver. Wise and lyrical, yet given to fits of inspired, freewheeling foolishness, *Old Souls & Wolf Tickets* is a genuine musical contradiction. But what else would one expect from the world's most popular purveyor of "alternative jive?"

"It's discombobulated jive, that's what I'd call it," Weiss says, describing his new record. "There's some blues, some New Orleans-type stuff, some sentimental stuff. I'd say it's the closest we've ever gotten to getting the live show on record. We like to be coordinated, you know? We don't want to do any layers or overdubs. It just seems to have more integrity doing it this way."

For more information, please contact Sheryl Northrop at [phone number, e-mail address] or Mike King at [phone number, e-mail address].

Digital Servicing vs. Physical Servicing

Music publicists are moving into digital servicing for promos/ advance music, but it's usually on a case-by-case scenario. Publicists that are working albums that they expect writers to be excited about often do 100 percent digital servicing. As an example, the large independent label Beggars Banquet e-mails a unique code to writers, which leads them to a Web site where they enter the code and then download a full album and a press kit. However, not all writers are adapting to digital servicing, and for new artists, a press kit should still contain the physical essentials: a CD, a press release, and press quotes. Again, all photos are sent digitally all the time. Photos are never serviced to writers anymore unless they are photocopied within the press kit.

COMMON PROBLEMS WITH PROMO KITS

Be sure to avoid the following in your press kit:

- *Too Much* **Information.** There is no reason to have a dozen pages describing the conditions under which you recorded the record, your political leanings, what all of the songs are about, etc. The biographical information in your press kit should be informational and concise.

- **Poor Grammar.** Misspelling the recipient's name on your package or cover letter is a big no-no. And while it may be acceptable to avoid punctuation and capitalization in instant messages to your friends, it is definitely NOT acceptable when you are writing to someone asking them to review your record.

- **Overreaching Package.** Again, there is no need to create some grand package to really "wow" the recipient. If the music and/or story isn't any good, it really doesn't matter if you include tchotchkes in with your press kit.

- *Not Enough* **Information.** You covered all your grammar bases, your music is hot, you addressed it to the right person, you've got some momentum, and the writer is interested in finding out more. But wait, who are you? It may seem obvious, but always be sure to put your contact info all over the package. Writers may not be the most organized crew in the world, and things can easily get sepa- rated. Clearly mark your name on the CD, on your bio— even drop some business cards in the package.

- **Poor Research/No Prior Contact.** It's fundamental that you send your kit to the right person. Never address your press kit "To whom it may concern." Find out who the right person is through a phone call. We'll talk more in depth about this later on, but in addition to knowing the name of the person to send to, you also have to be aware of what kind of music the publication writes about.

- **Bad Tone.** Another big turnoff is a promo kit with a demanding tone. Remember, the goal of the kit is to present your band and your music in the best possible light, and the language you use is important. Be nice. We received thousands of demo submissions at Ryko (which we tried our best to keep up with). We once received a promo kit from twin sisters who sang folk music. Not only was the cover letter off-putting in tone (along the lines of reprimanding the label for not already knowing that they are the Next Big Thing!), they demanded we send the kit back after we reviewed it! Bad form.

THE IMPORTANCE OF A PRESS STORY

Music writers have it tough. Not only do they get inundated with more information than a human is designed to comprehend, but they are under the added pressure of writing about music, which is one of the more difficult topics to describe using words. Good music writers are always searching for ways to differentiate their reviews and features from the multitude of other reviews out there. The famous *Rolling Stone* writer Lester Bangs was fired by publisher Jann Wenner for being "disrespectful to musicians," but his unorthodox writing style and ability to create a story around a record is legendary. (He is credited for coining the term "punk" in a negative review of the MC5's *Kick Out the Jams* record in 1970.) It's essential that you help writers create their story. For an artist or publicist, a creative story provides the "foot in the door" that is necessary to elevate their relationship with the music writers to the next step: having them listen to the music to decide if it is worthy to review on its own merits.

A successful press story accomplishes a couple of things:

- It fulfills a basic need the music writers have: making the release interesting. Plus, writers are pressed for time, and have been known to cut and paste directly from a press release. Make it easy for them by handing them a creative story that they can personalize and make their own.

- A good story provides the writers with a point of reference. Lines like "In the tradition of Buck Owens" let writers know immediately what to expect from your music before they even listen to it. Anything that helps to speed up the understanding of what the record sounds like and why it is interesting helps.

- A good press story can also relate what you do to a current event. Because they are so busy and are always trying to narrow down their "to write" pile, writers will use any excuse they can to *not* write about something, and if they consider your record, your music, or your story old news, you are going to have problems. As an example, MC Lars got a good amount of publicity and radio play a few years back with his "Download This Song" release. The song was great commentary on the current state of the music industry at the time, when downloading music was in all the major headlines.

Let's look at a couple examples of effective press stories.

A Press Story in Action: Korn Go Green

Almost every piece of news you read about a band began its life as a press release. Korn, an established band eight records into their career, led their press charge for a recent record with a release touting the band's eco-friendly tour. Here's the headline, which ran on MTV.com:

Korn Go Green: Band Concocts Own Biofuel, Korntastic; Converts to Biodiesel for Tour

"We can't change the world, but we can all make a difference," says front man Jonathan Davis.

Korn's publicity team at Virgin created an event at Times Square where they announced their intention to "go green" on their tour to support the new record. Though a new recording is big news, "going green" is even bigger because it's less usual. Big bands release CDs every day, but bands do not "go green" every day. Without a doubt, this event was preceded by a press release, which was likely reprinted verbatim by MTV.com. The story on MTV.com continues:

In addition, Korn—whose untitled eighth studio album lands in stores Tuesday (July 31)—discussed Korntastic, their own recipe for biofuel, which they're working on with MusicMatters' Sustainable Minded Artists Recording and Touring program. The formula, according to the band's publicist, is still in development and will be revealed soon via Korn's new Web site, korntastic.com.

The mention of the record release date, and the giveaway line, "As reported by the band's publicist," is the clear indication that this piece of news was taken directly from a press release.

Even though the record has been panned by music critics ("Korn's new album has a lot more missing than just a title," writes the

Cleveland Plain Dealer), the publicity department succeeded in getting major coverage and record detail information out prior to release date by orchestrating an interesting news story that just happened to be related to Korn's new album and upcoming tour.

A Press Story in Action: Lori McKenna and the Family Angle

The greater Boston area has a healthy folk music community rotating around Club Passim in Harvard Square. At one point, a single manager worked with three key players in the folk music scene, one of them being Lori McKenna. Her story was great: local musician from a Boston suburb, a self-described house-wife and the mother of five kids that got into music later in her life. She self-released three records with the same press angle: Singer, Songwriter, Wife, and Mother. Around the time of her third release, I began seeing some more major local visibility including a front-page living arts piece in the *Boston Globe* written by Joan Anderman—the top-tier music writer for the *Globe*—with the same angle: "Songwriter Juggles Career with Demands of Everyday Family Life."

In 2006, Superstar Faith Hill included three of McKenna's songs on her number 1 album *Fireflies*. Warner Brothers scooped Lori up later that year. In Warner's bio on her site, her story and angle are the same as what I have heard for the past ten years:

> *Lori McKenna is a mother of five from Stoughton, Mass. (pop. 27,000), about 20 miles outside Boston. There, she lives quietly—well, as quietly as a house with five children can get—with her husband of 18 years, Gene, a plumber for the local gas company. For years, she drove her kids to school in a 1999 Ford Windstar minivan with 150,000 miles on it. It is fitting Lori entitled her Warner Brothers debut album **Unglamorous**.*
>
> *McKenna began performing at open-mic nights in Boston, and the enthusiastic response led to her own shows. Finding it perfectly natural to balance her full home life with a burgeoning musical career, she took care of the kids all day, played shows in the evening, and wrote songs at the kitchen table after the children's bedtime. She drove from show to show in the same minivan in which she ferried around her kids, who now range in age from 2 to 17. "I'm just a housewife from Stoughton who likes to write songs," McKenna says.*

INSIDER TIP: PUBLICITY VS. PROMOTION

There are plenty of ambiguous terms in the record industry, and it's important to note the difference between publicity and promotion, two major segments. While a publicist might promote an artist to his/her contacts at press, the term record promotion actually refers to the people that work records to radio. Basically, if you want to work with a company to promote your music to press, you work with a publicity company, and if you want to work with someone to help you at radio, you would hire a promotion company.

The confusion doesn't end there. Although publicists work your record to their online and offline press contacts, they also cover some ground in the radio world, too. Traditionally, NPR (National Public Radio) is considered a press target, not a radio target. NPR runs music press stories and artist interviews, and is pitched in the same way that a print outlet would be pitched.

DETERMINING YOUR PRESS OUTLETS: PRINT, RADIO, TV, AND ONLINE

PR outlets are broken into several different segments. Writers are fickle and are under varying deadlines, so depending on the publication and its print schedule, a publicist may have to approach them at different times in the lifecycle of a project, and with different information. For example, many major monthly music outlets won't review a record after street date, but might write about a great live show post-release. When you are creating your press outreach plan, you need to consider the following outlets.

Print

Major National Entertainment Outlets

Major national entertainment outlets are the gold standard of print publications. These pubs have a tremendous national reach. They might be looking for the Lori McKenna-esque human-interest stories that can affect people across a very broad demographic, they might be looking for a "trend" story, or they might just hop on the bandwagon of the latest major label record coverage. Things are going well if you are getting positive responses from these outlets. This is the highest echelon of print publicity.

Examples of national entertainment outlets include:

- *GQ*
- *USA Today*
- *Entertainment Weekly*
- *People*
- *Wired*
- *Newsweek*
- *Vanity Fair*
- *Time*
- *US Weekly*
- *New Yorker*
- *Playboy*
- *Interview*
- *Details*
- *Esquire*

National Music Magazines

Most national music magazines have their own specific niche: *American Songwriter* out of Nashville is more alt-country, *Magnet* leans more indie, *AP* is more hard rock, and so on.

Examples of national music mags include:

- *Rolling Stone*
- *Spin*
- *Magnet*
- *Mean*
- *Performing Songwriter*
- *American Songwriter*
- *Alternative Press*

Genre Specific Magazines

There are a number of pubs that tailor exclusively to certain genres of music. For example, if you were a blues artist, you would focus on specific outlets like *Blues Review* magazine.

Regional

Regional outlets serve a few purposes. First, they are great outlets for record reviews prior to release. Second, they are very interested in the same sort of human interest or trend stories that the major nationals are interested in. Lastly, they are perfect for show previews and reviews. Because of these diverse functions, regional outlets are often approached on several different occasions throughout the marketing life cycle of a record.

Some top markets and their associated regional publications:

- Boston *(Globe, Herald, Phoenix, Dig)*
- Chicago *(Sun Times, Tribune)*
- Denver *(Post, Denver Westword)*
- New York City *(Daily News, Post, New York Times, NY Observer)*
- Philadelphia *(Inquirer, Daily News)*
- San Francisco *(Chronicle, SF Gate, Guardian)*
- Seattle *(Weekly, Time Out)*

College/Zine

College pubs and 'zines (again, short for fanzine, a small press publication or alternative newsletter) are great outlets for artists that have a younger-skewing audience. Artists that are playing the college circuit and getting college radio airplay (more on that in the next chapter) would be wise to follow up with college paper press to complete the full court press on that demo. 'Zines often have low circulation numbers but tend to have readers that are music fanatics. While many 'zines have made the jump to blogs over the past few years, there are still some great print outlets for genre-specific 'zine exposure, including: *Big Takeover, Chunklet,* and *Giant Robot.*

In terms of college coverage, there are some aggregators that one could work with to target many college pubs at once, like Hear/Say and U-Wire. But if your band has a college tour scheduled, it makes sense to laser in on and target the pubs in and around the schools you're playing.

For example, target college publications for an east coast tour run could include:

- University of Vermont: *Vermont Cynic*
- University of New Hampshire: *The New Hampshire*

- University of Massachusetts at Amherst: *Daily Collegian*
- Boston University: *Daily Free Press*
- Northeastern University: *Northeastern News*
- Harvard University: *Crimson*
- Massachusetts Institute of Technology: *The Tech*
- Boston College: *The Heights*
- Tufts University: *Daily*
- University of Massachusetts: Boston: *Mass Media*
- Brandeis University: *The Justice*
- Yale University: *Daily News*
- University of Connecticut: *Daily Campus*
- Wesleyan University: *Argus*
- Dartmouth University: *The Dartmouth*
- Bates College: *Student*
- University of Southern Maine: *Free Press*
- Brown University: *Daily Herald*
- University of Rhode Island: *The Good 5 Cent Cigar*
- Rhode Island College: *The Anchor*
- New York University: *Washington Square News*
- Ithaca College: *The Ithacan*
- Colgate University: *The Colgate Maroon-News*
- Rutgers University: *Daily Targum*
- Cornell University: *Daily Sun*

HOW TO PITCH PRINT MEDIA

After you've identified the print publications that are most appropriate for your music or your tour dates, you need to connect with the folks that are actually doing the writing for these pubs. An up-to-date media database of names and addresses is the cornerstone of a good press campaign. Almost all print publications have a masthead, which is the section up front that lists the publisher, editor, art director, and writers. Take a look through the magazine, identify the writer that has written about music similar to yours, and send them a copy of your press kit. A lot of pubs also use freelance writers. If you find the name of a writer in the reviews section that is not listed in the masthead, call the magazine and see if you can get the address of that specific

writer. If the writer has a good track record of bringing interesting music reviews to the publication, they might be able to
pitch a review of your record to the editor as a freelancer. Lastly,
many pubs have Web sites that list e-mail contact info. Find the
proper writer, and send a respectful e-mail inquiring about their
submission policy.

INSIDER TIP: RECORD RELEASE PRESS VS. TOUR PRESS

A good music publicity campaign is focused on two distinct press segments with two
different goals: Prerelease press leading up to the record's street date is mostly focused
on record reviews and features, and if you are a massive artist or really connecting with
press, television appearances to support the upcoming release. Once the release date
hits, the press campaign is less focused on reviews (as mentioned, pubs rarely review a
record post street date), and more focused on supporting tour dates, or larger "trend"
stories.

Television/Radio

Television and certain radio outlets are considered press terri-
tory, and the major players (Letterman, Conan, Leno, etc.) are
solicited in the same manner as other top-tier major national
entertainment outlets. While it's somewhat easier to get in-studio
performances together with regional TV outlets, national TV
outlets will only feature artists that are either already established or have an incredible buzz. NPR has several programs that
feature interviews and stories on musicians. *Fresh Air*, hosted
by Terry Gross, is a notable example. *Car Talk* also takes car-
themed submissions as bumper music (a term used to describe
the short clips of music that buffer transitions between programming elements, like when a program "goes to commercial").

Here's a list of some of the more sought-after radio and television
press outlets:

- *Letterman, Conan, Saturday Night Live*
- *CBS Saturday* or *Sunday Morning*
- NPR (*Fresh Air, Morning Edition, All Things Considered*)
- *Westwood One, KCRW Morning Becomes Eclectic*
- *Good Day L.A.* (example of a regional TV program)

Blogs/Online Music Sites

Music blogs are incredibly influential press outlets. Sites like Pitch-
forkmedia.com can make or break a record. For example, because

of a 0.0 review from Pitchfork, some independent retailers initially refused to stock the Travis Morrison records in their stores!

INSIDER TIP: EXCLUSIVE MATERIAL

Blogs *love* exclusive material. Keep some tracks and video free for blog and online outreach. (iTunes loves exclusive tracks, too!)

How to Pitch Blogs

While many of the same concepts that you apply to traditional media are used when you pitch blogs (be relevant!), the process by which you pitch them and the information that they require is slightly different than the way you would approach traditional media. Many blogs are staffed by only one or two folks that are simply die-hard music fans. (Pitchfork is an exception, and operates more like a traditional magazine.) They admire folks that send them personalized messages, and abhor cut and paste "templatized" outreach. They appreciate those that have taken the time to read their blog, comment on it, and get involved.

Blogs generally run quick-hit pieces, and don't have the time or space to print a full press release. If you can summarize the press release and provide a link to the release elsewhere, you'll have much better luck. Also: be persistent. It can take a bit of door-knocking to get a blog relationship off the ground.

INDEPENDENT PUBLICISTS

The music business revolves around connections. Of course, favors, dinners and drinks, and secret handshakes are rife throughout any industry. But perhaps because of the sheer volume of music that is being created and in need of promotional support, the decision makers in the music industry more often than not rely on trusted sources to help them decide what artists to promote, rather than promoting artists based on the merits of the music itself. In many cases, you need a foot in the door to be taken seriously and to make national press headway.

This is where independent publicists come in. Independent publicists (indies) have a database of contacts, and more importantly, they have personal relationships with many of the influential writers and freelancers. A good publicist is aware of trend stories that writers are looking for, is an expert in pitching music, and is exceptional in crafting press releases and finding a "hook" that writers will grab onto.

INSIDER TIP: PITCH LETTER

Here's an example of a successful pitch made on behalf of Artists House Music to the editor of *Wired's* music blog (who's contact info was easily found on his blog), and his response.

From: Michael King

Date: Wed, 20 Aug 2008 12:24:06 -0400

To: Eliot Van Buskirk

Subject: John Simson / SoundExchange Video Interview

Hi Eliot,

I'm the managing editor of an online musicians resource called www.artistshousemusic.org. I'm a big fan of your *Wired* blog, and I thought you might be interested in a video interview with John Simson from SoundExchange that we created a couple months back.

The link is here:

http://www.artistshousemusic.org/videos/soundexchange+head+john+simson+on+we

bcasting+the+future+of+radio+and+the+day+the+music+died

Might be timely for you in terms of the *Washington Post* piece with Pandora, and I know you are completely on top of all the happenings with the CRB and SoundExchange.

Keep up the great work!

Mike

From: Eliot Van Buskirk

Date: Wed, 20 Aug 2008 18:10:42 -0400

To: Michael King

Subject: Re: John Simson / SoundExchange Video Interview

Excellent -- thanks, Michael. I posted something here:

http://blog.wired.com/music/2008/08/soundexchange-h.html

Cheers,

evb

http://blog.wired.com/music

When You Need an Indie Publicist

It's expensive anytime you hire outside help. If you're just starting out, it makes sense to try your hand with the local and regional press and get a feel for how the process works. But if you've got a solid following already and want to break through to a larger crowd in support of a tour or new record (and you have the budget to do it), it makes sense to hire an expert.

What to Look for in an Indie Publicist and How to Find One

Publicists run the gamut, in terms of coverage. Some specialize in particular genres and some work with artists in many genres and have a more national reach. The number 1 thing to look for in an indie publicist is the result of a project that closely resembles your own. For example, the press surrounding the last two Black Keys records was outstanding. NPR, *Rolling Stone, the New York Times, Time*, Letterman, Conan, Pitchfork, quotes from Robert Plant, Thom Yorke (Radiohead)—the press was everywhere! It helps that the band is undeniably awesome, but their publicity firm was absolutely on fire promoting the record. If your band has a similar sound to the Black Keys ("If Led Zeppelin had formed in 1955 and recorded for Chess Records, they'd probably sound a lot like the Black Keys." *—Rolling Stone*), it makes sense to see who is working the record and connect with them. Publicists want to be found. A quick Internet search turns up the fact that Carla Sacks at Sacks and Co. is working the Black Keys.

Sacks and Co. is a big player in the indie press world. Other major publicists you should be aware of include:

- Big Hassle: runs the gamut from Crowded House to Gillian Welch

- Nasty Little Man: has worked some big name jam band artists like Dave Matthews, Trey Anastasio, and Medeski Martin & Wood

- Cary Baker at Conqueroo: currently working the Stax Records relaunch

- Merlis for Hire: Bob Merlis has been around for a while, and works with some old-school legendary artists: Mellencamp, ZZ Top, the Rolling Stones reissues from ABKCO

What a Publicist Looks for in You

A publicist's effectiveness is based on their relationship with writers. When a writer sees a package from a publicist that has brought them great music in the past, they are much more inclined to put that package at the top of their "to listen to" pile. Over and above everything else, good publicists need the music they work to be fantastic. Bad indie publicists might shill anything by anyone that will pay them, but a good indie will refuse projects that they feel will tarnish their image or reputation. Beyond having the foundation set with great music, indies are looking to be a part of the momentum of a project. Maybe it's a great set at the South by Southwest festival (SXSW), maybe it is a huge word-of-mouth groundswell, but if a publicist has something to build on, it makes their job infinitely easier. Being a great musician and having a great record is one thing, but publicists are always looking for the hook to grab the attention of the writer and make them want to listen to the record.

INSIDER TIP: KEEP IT RECENT AND CLEAN

Publicists tend to stay away from folks that talk trash about their previous publicity companies (they know that you might have the same things to say about them!), and they tend to stay away from projects that have already been out for a long time.

What a Publicist Can and Can't Do

Publicists cannot guarantee coverage. What they can do is package and pitch an artist with the goal of getting a writer's attention, have them listen to the record, and then decide if it is worthy to cover on its own merits. A good publicist will make a writer or editor want to learn more about you, and provide reasons why they should give you some editorial.

How Long You Should Hire Them For

Lead time is incredibly important in the press world. Major national outlets are sometimes finalizing content four months prior to running it. If you are hiring a publicist for a record release campaign designed to draw major national press, four to six months is pretty standard.

How They Charge and How Much They Charge

Publicists usually charge on a per-month basis. Prices vary widely, but tend to be in the range of $750 (green publicist, or limited coverage) to $5,000 (top-tier major national coverage) per month. Publicists also typically charge you for expenses (postage costs, copies, etc.), which vary from publicist to publicist.

Reporting

Publicists should provide weekly reporting to you. The report should include whom they contacted, when they contacted them, notes on the conversation, and all positive leads/confirmed placements.

INSIDER TIP: THE SQUEAKY WHEEL TECHNIQUE

When you hire a publicist, you need to enter the relationship with the knowledge that you are likely one of many projects that the publicist is working on. Be vigilant in overseeing your publicist, and work with them on ideas and passing them new information they can use to help tell your story. Being the squeaky wheel to your indie is a good way to be sure that they are indeed working your record above the others that they may also be representing.

INTERVIEW: SONYA KOLOWRAT, PUBLICIST FOR THE BEGGARS GROUP

Sonya Kolowrat is a national publicist at the Beggars Group of Labels, and works with artists on 4AD, XL Recordings, and Rough Trade. Her recent press campaigns include Vampire Weekend, the National, Blonde Redhead, and Scott Walker. She began her PR career in 1995 at Rykodisc where she worked with artists in many different genres including Cubanismo, Nick Drake, Morphine, and Bill Hicks. Prior to Beggars, Sonya helmed the indie PR company Midnight Feeding.

When pitching a new release, what is a writer looking for from a publicist? How do you excite writers and get them into what you are working on?

You really need to give them a reason to listen and make it easy for them. An interesting angle is ideal, so not just "Joe Blow has recorded a new record and here it is," but "Joe Blow just finished touring with Radiohead, and he was handpicked by them to open, and *Rolling Stone* called him 'the next Nick Drake.'" Obviously everyone wants the music to stand on its own, and maybe it will, but these are people getting 300 albums a week, and they need a reason to put yours in the CD player/iPod, etc.

I think they want basic, brief, easily digestible info, *not* a four-page bio. That will likely go in the garbage. I think it's great if you have the ability to send a link to an MP3 they can stream or download—something they can listen to right away with the click of a mouse. Quotes from other publications are helpful, including a few prominent foreign publications. Also if a week or so after your initial pitch something great happens, let them know in a personal e-mail, things like being number one at a top radio station, or getting a late-night TV booking, or an amazing review somewhere. Don't bombard them with info. Be selective.

It's also *really* important to know whom you are pitching. Know your writer and your publication. Know the lead time in relation to your release. Don't try to get a record review in *Spin* a week before an album comes out, and don't pitch a writer that writes exclusively about metal with your folk singer. Do your research. It's really easy these days to find out what writers write about what kind of music. Go to some Web sites of bands you think sound like the band you're working with and see who has written about them, and make sure they are aware/get a copy.

What makes for an effective release?

I try to keep it under one page, kind of like a résumé. If people read them at all, they want to know the key info fast.

How can independent musicians find the proper contacts for print media?

Think of the kind of magazines that would be the most likely to write about your music, go buy them, and copy the masthead. All the contact info is usually in there or can be found on the publication's Web site. Read the magazine, and be well informed of the sections and which writer is writing about which kinds of music.

How important are blogs to the overall press picture? Are blogs becoming more of a tastemaker vehicle than traditional print media?

Blogs are very important these days in helping to create a buzz. I think they are most effective in the early part of a campaign. If the blogs like a band, they will make it the talk of the town. Hopefully the hype matches the quality of the record! I think the blog support fuels the fire for other coverage. TV bookers and magazine editors are paying a lot of attention to what the blogs write about, and it definitely affects what they cover.

What press outlets have you seen yield the best results?

It depends on the goal. If you want to sell a ton of records, your best bet is NPR and national television like *CBS Saturday Morning*. Big features in glossy magazines don't sell a lot of records, but they will help get your records in stores. Late night TV sometimes gets you a sales spike, but it's more of a prestige thing. If a band is on tour, then press in local media is key for selling out the show and building regional awareness. So, it depends on the project, whether the band tours, and the goals. If your goal is just to create awareness and buzz, online media is the way to go.

When should a developing artist consider hiring an independent publicist?

In terms of timing, artists should consider an indie when they have a full-length album that is completed and four or five months away from being in stores or available online. Having a national community, label and/or distribution is important, too. A publicist will get you press coverage, but if people want to buy your record, it needs to be available easily for the interested reader. Artists should also consider: (1) an indie's price per month vs. what you can afford, (2) how many months you want to hire them for, with three months prior to release being ideal for long-lead press and usually the minimum, and (3) how many other projects they are working on at the same time. You are better off with someone with a small roster that can dedicate time for you, rather than a huge company who is working your band and forty others at the same time.

I think looking at magazines, taking notes on what artists you are reading about a lot, and finding out who does their press is a good indicator of who is doing a good job. You should like the other artists on the indie's roster, and ideally, you should be familiar with them. I would suggest talking to several companies and getting references from other artists. It's like hiring a nanny for your baby! You need to trust this person and trust their judgment and opinions.

What are some things a band can do to generate interest in their release?

A band should have a mailing list, a MySpace page, and a Web site that is frequently updated with news, tour dates, and streaming audio. They should actively be in touch with their fans. The band should also provide a wide selection of press photos and a comprehensive bio as well.

What should an artist consider when creating their press photos? What works and what doesn't?

First of all, there is no need for hard photos anymore. It's all done digitally now. There is also no need for black-and-white photos. An ideal photo is one where you can see all the member's faces, and they are *not* far in the distance. They should also *not* just be standing in front of a wall. Getting somewhat creative is ideal. Have the singer behind a bar and the rest of the band be the bar's patron's, or have them doing something interesting—anything, really. Just don't stand them up against a wall!

Summary

Press outreach is a fundamental component of any marketing plan. Identifying the proper outlets, creating effective releases targeted to your goals, understanding how writers prefer to receive information, and knowing when (and who!) to hire to help you makes a big difference in the success of any press campaign.

Workshop

Create a draft for the press component of your marketing plan.
Answer the following questions:

- Briefly describe your press story. In what ways can you
  differentiate yourself? How can you make your story interesting to writers?

- Based on this story and your demographics, what outlets
  make sense to target? If you are a touring band, what local/
  regional outlets will you target?

- Do you feel it is appropriate to work with an independent
  publicist? If so, which one might you target and why?

9 Radio Promotion

*"It is a riddle, wrapped in a mystery, inside an enigma;
but perhaps there is a key."* —Winston Churchill

While Churchill may have been referring to the uncertain
motives of Russia at the time, this quote also perfectly encompasses radio promotion as it exists today.

To many artists, labels, and marketers, traditional radio really
is an enigma. High-profile radio campaigns aimed at exposing
artists to commercial radio can run into the hundreds of thousands of dollars. *Payola*—the illegal act of "pay for play," in the
forms of cash, trips, and other bribes—appears to be alive and
well. (Sony agreed to pay more than $10 million as a result of a
2005 payola investigation by former New York State Attorney
General Eliot L. Spitzer.) But as Churchill says, there is a key.
Certain radio formats, stations, and shows continue to be effective marketing vehicles for developing artists.

HOW RADIO WORKS

In a perfect world, radio stations across the country would play
songs based simply on the merits of the songs themselves. In
a perfect world, a major radio station in a major market could
be solicited in the same fashion as a publicist solicits *Rolling
Stone*: by sending a package, making a follow-up call, and if the
"deciders" (in the case of radio, the program directors) like what
they hear, they would promote the record by playing it on air.
Unfortunately, this is not how large traditional radio stations
work. Traditional radio is (still) a big business, and there is a
huge promotional vehicle behind any song you hear played on
commercial radio. (*Commercial radio* is a term used to describe a
form of radio in the U.S. and several other countries: those that
are broadcasting for profit.) The amount of money and resources
it takes to get music played on commercial radio during peak
listening times makes it an unrealistic avenue to almost all independent artists and labels.

The good news is that there are a number of noncommercial
traditional radio stations that are a completely viable outlet
for a musician that does not have a spare $500,000 to drop on
a commercial radio campaign. (*Noncommercial* describes those

stations that are not funded by advertising, typically located on the left side of the radio dial.) Additionally, commercial stations often have specialty shows that fall outside of their regular programming that are open to less expensive solicitation. Online and satellite radio have further opened the doors to independent artists and labels, and provided another avenue for artists who aren't on major labels to get national/international radio coverage.

Before we get into all of this, let's take a step back and talk about what needs to be happening with your band before you consider radio support.

WHEN SHOULD YOU CONSIDER RADIO SUPPORT?

Traditional terrestrial radio (as opposed to online or satellite radio, which have their own sets of rules) should be the last consideration in an independent artist's marketing campaign for a few reasons. First, it can be incredibly expensive. Second, there are fewer openings available to promote new artists than there are at other marketing outlets (like press, retail, online, and touring), which makes it incredibly difficult to get play during the time of day when most people actually listen to the radio (as opposed to placement at 3:00 A.M.). Third, and most importantly, radio is best used to support other efforts you already have in place—in particular, a tour.

For example, say you are a New York City–based band, and you've hired an indie radio promoter. They've secured radio play at KUSF, a great noncommercial station in San Francisco. Without a tour in that market, without records in the stores in that market, and without press visibility, the radio play will not really do you much good.

Some folks (independent radio promoters, usually) feel that radio play should come before a distribution deal or other marketing, as it can be used as a "promotional ammunition" to sell the distributor or a label on the merits of your band. While there is some truth to this, distributors these days are just as impressed by a solid online community, great press, and a band that can draw a good amount of fans to their shows around the country. Radio on a national level is a more expensive and generally less effective avenue, if your goal is to impress distributors or labels.

A national radio campaign should not be considered the "magic bullet" to kick-start your career or marketing campaign. However, depending on where you are with your career, your fan base, and your general visibility, some degree of radio presence can help to propel your visibility into larger arenas.

What Else Should Be in Place Prior to Considering Your Radio Campaign?

To truly capitalize on a radio promotional campaign, both at noncommercial and commercial radio, it's best to have your integrated marketing campaign running on all cylinders. Radio is designed to complement your other marketing efforts and make the listeners take action.

Web Presence. To start, you'll need to have your Web site up and optimized with tour dates, any press you've had, bio, a mailing list, etc.—everything we talked about in chapter 6. If folks hear about you through a local specialty radio show and are intrigued, chances are they'll search for you online.

Community and Integrated Marketing Plan. Again, touring, press, a distribution campaign, and most importantly a growing fan base should also be in place before you undertake your radio campaign. It makes the radio pitches a lot easier if you (or your radio promo indie, to be more specific) can point out that a buzz is happening with your campaign. These other segments help folks hear your music, find your music in stores, find out where you're playing, see you live, and become converted into true fans.

Money. If you do decide to undertake a radio promotion campaign, you are going to need to budget for creating and sending a number of promos (promotional copies) of your record to your target stations. This is a serious consideration for an artist on a limited budget.

HOW A TERRESTRIAL (BRICK-AND-MORTAR) RADIO STATION IS STRUCTURED

If you feel the time is right for you to go for radio visibility, your first step is understanding how a station operates and who is involved in its various functions.

The program director (at commercial radio) and the music director (at noncommercial radio) are the main contacts for promoting a new record to radio. The typical staff of a radio station includes:

- Disc Jockey. This is the on-air personality you hear during any regular programming or broadcast. In the case of noncommercial radio, the DJ often has the editorial freedom to play what he or she likes. But in a commercial radio situation, the DJ has far less autonomy.

- Specialty Show Host. The specialty show host runs a dedicated type of show, usually weekly, for the station (i.e., a blues brunch on Sunday, or a local artist show on Sunday evening). These shows are typically on the weekend or off hours on the weekdays.

- Music Director. At commercial radio, the music director works for the program director to determine what gets played and at what time. In many cases within the noncommercial world, the music director oversees all the music that is selected.

- Program Director. The program director decides who and what goes on air. He or she oversees all the DJs who work for the station as well. The program director is usually the person at the station that labels and independent radio promoters talk to when they promote new releases.

- Sales Staff. Commercial stations have a staff of folks selling on-air ads.

- General Manager. The GM oversees the entire operation.

HOW NONCOMMERCIAL RADIO WORKS

What Is Noncommercial Radio?

There are roughly 2,000 noncommercial stations in the U.S. playing new music. These stations are broken into three main segments:

- college radio stations

- community/public stations

- NPR (National Public Radio) stations

Noncommercial stations are a completely valid option for an independent musician or label that has reached a point in their career where radio visibility makes sense (for all the reasons outlined above). The cost of entry to work with the noncommercial stations is reasonable, there are generally more options for new music. Major labels tend to ignore them, and unlike commercial radio, music really is played based on the personal preference of the DJ or music director. College radio makes up the bulk of the noncommercial stations in the U.S. and Canada.

How College Radio Works

College radio stations run the gamut, in terms of size. Some stations have limited power and only reach the college's dorms, while other stations are some of the most powerful in the area, and have a big effect on sales and visibility in their region. As an example, Georgia State's college radio station, WRAS, transmits on 100,000 watts (very powerful and far-reaching, comparable to some commercial radio transmissions). Additionally, KCRW, the college station associated with Santa Monica Community College in California, is one of the most influential stations in the country for breaking new music, across any radio format. Artists that have been "broken" by that station (in particular, broken by the show *Morning Becomes Eclectic*) include Coldplay and Beck.

The DJs and the music directors at college stations are made up of students (and in some cases, local volunteers, or paid employees) that are on air to fulfill credits for courses. Generally, each student creates a one-hour playlist (under the supervision of the music director) comprised of whatever they feel like playing: new music, old music, live performances, interviews, etc. Presently, college stations generally prefer more "alternative" or "indie" leaning music. (75 percent of the music played on college radio could be classified as such.)

What Is CMJ and Why Does It Matter?

CMJ (College Radio Journal) publishes *CMJ New Music Report*, a weekly magazine that reports the playlists of hundreds of college stations from around the country. The music directors for each individual CMJ-reporting station submit their weekly "top 30" list of artists to CMJ. (Not all college stations report to CMJ, but the better-run ones generally do.) The top 200 CMJ artists are compiled by taking an averaging of the artists that are played the most frequently at college stations around the country, and also taking into account the "weight" of the stations who are playing them. Larger stations are weighted more heavily and are perceived as more influential than smaller stations. For example, one spin at a higher weight station such as KALX (University of California, Berkeley, CA) is "worth more" than a spin at KMSU in Mankato, MN.

"CMJ's Top 200" is their most popular chart, and provides the best indication of the most popular music played at college radio nationally. Other charts include the "Radio Select" chart, which is a chart compiling the playlists of the hundred largest college radio stations, the "Radio 200 Adds" chart, which compiles the highest "added" artists (meaning added into the music library at a station, which does not necessarily mean it will be played), and several genre-specific charts including Loud Rock, RPM (which covers electronic music), Hip-Hop, Jazz, New World, Triple A (Adult Album Alternative—mostly singer-songwriters), Latin Alternative, and Internet Broadcast.

More than anything, the CMJ charts are useful insofar as they provide a point of reference for your college radio promotional campaign's success. From a marketing perspective, bands can use the information in the charts to help hone in on their regional outreach. Clubs and retailers nationally are often tied in with their local college station. Additionally, CMJ is read by decision makers within the industry: labels, club bookers, and press indies. Records that are charting there provide these "tastemakers" with an idea of up-and-coming bands.

However, this information isn't cheap. While their Web site has some basic info, the extensive details can only be found in the New Music Report, available at a yearly subscription rate of $395 in the U.S., and $795 outside of the U.S., or via an online paid subscription.

How Noncommercial Community/Public Radio Works

In addition to the college radio stations, noncommercial also extends to community and public radio. Public radio tends to favor less "aggressive" (read: softer) artists and music than their younger compatriots at college radio. These noncommercial stations have fewer paid staff than their commercial radio counterparts, and with the stations that focus on a particular genre of music (like WPFW in Washington D.C., for example, which focuses on jazz), there may be only one music director that oversees all the station's music programming. Many noncommercial public radio stations have specialty shows that focus on everything from exotica to children's music.

MARKETING TO NONCOMMERCIAL RADIO

Similar to regional press outreach, it's completely possible to conduct a noncommercial regional radio campaign yourself, if you have the time to do the research, outreach, and follow-up. Noncommercial stations are listener supported and make it easy for you to find them online. A simple Web search can easily pull up listings of all the noncommercial stations in a particular area, and in many cases, the station's playlists and the names and contact info of the music directors are readily available online. The trick is finding out which stations host the shows that make the most sense to your particular type of music.

National noncommercial campaigns are a bit trickier to handle yourself. First of all, depending on what your goal is, you have to service perhaps 300 to 500 stations at once (which is also the size of the mailing you're looking at if you are trying to "chart" on CMJ). Once you've done the mailing, you then need to reach out to each of these stations with a phone call (preferably) or e-mail to be sure they got the CD, pitch the music directors about your music, and ask them what's happening with the CD: have they added it to the library? Are they spinning it? What else do they think? This follow-up often needs to happen for several weeks in order for you to get the support you need for an effective campaign.

Additionally, half the battle of getting your music played on college radio is connecting with the college kids that staff the station. College kids have a whole lot going on outside of running their shows and choosing their playlists. Many music directors and DJs have office hours for taking calls (in theory!). If you are handling your college radio promotion campaign yourself, be sure to leave a message with the music director or DJ.

The workload of a national noncommercial campaign is usually too much for a band to undertake on its own, which is why independent radio promoters exist. More on this group shortly.

INSIDER TIP: THE GROWING COST OF DOING BUSINESS

In addition to the amount of time that a proper national radio campaign requires, the financial realities can be pretty daunting as well. Radio stations need to receive a proper CD in a package, with a one-sheet. It's also important that if you are going for college radio, you have other activities in place so that you can take advantage of the radio support. Here's a breakout of projected costs based on current USPS rates of $1.81 per CD package (cost of bubble mailer with postage for one CD).

There are about 1000 college stations that are eligible to send their playlists to CMJ. Say you are in a hip-hop band and want to get added to the Hip-Hop chart on CMJ. Three hundred stations report to this.

If you are sending CDs to CMJ, then you are likely touring as well. If you are touring, you want to support your dates by getting press visibility in key markets, as well as try for some national hip-hop pubs. Let's say you do a press mailing to 300 outlets to cover all major regional papers and targeted national media.

$1.81 x 600 CDs (300 for stations + 300 for the publicists)

= $1,086 for mailing costs.

You are likely going to want to hire an indie to help you at press and radio. Depending on your goals, how long your campaign is, and who you use, this could cost you anywhere from $1,000 to $4,000 for a radio campaign, and from $1,000 to $5,000 a month for three months of publicity coverage.

Based on these numbers, artists are looking at $12,000 to $15,000 (on the low end) to do an effective campaign to press and college radio using an indie!

HOW COMMERCIAL RADIO WORKS

Commercial radio rarely plays music by unsigned artists in their regular rotation. Even if you are signed to a major record label, the chances of getting significant radio play on large major-market (New York City, L.A., Chicago, San Francisco) stations are not great, even with a several hundred-thousand-dollar promotion budget.

You have to know things are not right in the commercial radio world when Lowry Mays, the founder of Clear Channel (one of the country's largest radio station's owner) busts out quotes like this: "If anyone said we were in the radio business, it wouldn't be someone from our company. We're not in the business of providing news and information. We're not in the business of providing well-researched music. We're simply in the business of selling our customers products."

There are many reasons why commercial radio won't play independent artists during regular rotation. As Mr. Mays eloquently mentions, at the top of the list is the fact that commercial stations are dependent on advertising revenue for their survival. Advertisers want to reach the broadest amount of listeners possible, and pay close attention to the Arbitron (a service that tracks the amount of listeners a station has, similar to the Nielsen service for that track's television viewership) numbers. Commercial stations cannot take the risk of alienating their listeners by introducing music that listeners might not be familiar with. Major label artists will likely have a national tour, national distribution, television visibility, press reviews, and an existing radio story—all elements that commercial radio needs to have happening before they will consider adding a song into rotation. And most importantly, major labels can spend $250,000 on the necessary indie radio promoters, $50,000 on the necessary trade ads, $50,000 on on-air ads, and so on.

Regular-rotation commercial-radio visibility can be viewed similarly to playing stadium shows on a tour. Whereas a band would not consider playing Madison Square Garden without the proper community and fan base in place to fill the seats, a band should also not consider a full commercial radio campaign without the momentum in place to draw in listeners.

Lastly, payola is apparently still alive and well. As we discussed, payola is the illegal practice of offering payment of other perks to radio stations in return for radio play. Although the government has taken steps at various times over the past fifty years to put an end to it (most notably, in 1960 with the Alan Freed scandal), the practice of major labels paying for airtime is still presently a part of the commercial radio promotion business.

There are specialty shows in many markets that play local music or specific genre-themed specialty shows on off hours, usually on weekends. As an example, the CBS-owned Active Rock (we'll explain this term in a minute) station in Boston, WBCN, airs Boston Emissions, a 2-hour local music show each Sunday night from 10 P.M. to 12 A.M. Additionally, there are a small number of commercial stations that focus on the Triple A and Americana formats, which are other possibilities for smaller labels and independent artists.

Commercial Radio Formats

Commercial radio stations are broken up into specific "formats." In radio-speak, "format" is the term used to describe the general style of music these stations play. There are roughly 10,000 commercial stations in the U.S., broken up into these main formats:

- Adult Album Alternative/Americana. Adult Album Alternative (Triple A), and Americana are the only radio formats that are found on both commercial and noncommercial stations. There are about 200 Triple A and Americana stations in the U.S. and Canada, and the formats are primarily focused on singer-songwriters who appeal to an older demographic. Popular current Triple A artists include folks like James Blunt, KT Tunstall, Bruce Springsteen, and Bryan Adams. The format has been morphing in recent years to include some "edgier" artists as well, such as Modest Mouse and Ben Harper. While still very difficult to reach, it is possible for independent labels to get visibility on Americana and Triple A radio.

- Top 40/Pop/Contemporary Hit Radio. These are the stations that play Pink, Justin Timberlake, and Britney Spears.

- Adult Contemporary. Adult contemporary (AC) radio encompasses the general "AC" format (Fergie, Gwen Stefani, John Mayer), as well as the "Hot AC" sub-format (generally a little more rocking: Maroon 5, Avril Lavigne, Goo Goo Dolls). AC is the most listened-to format, with roughly 1,500 stations, but they also have a limited capacity to play new music because of the high number of talk and sports programs scheduled.

- Country. There are over 2,000 country radio stations in the U.S. and Canada. Popular country radio artists include Kenny Chesney, Toby Keith, Garth Brooks, and Sugarland. A very difficult format for independent labels and artists to break into.

- Religious. Similar in size to country radio, this format encompasses Christian (Christian rock, Christian AC are popular examples), Gospel, Praise and Worship, and Ministry. Many religious stations are talk-based, and offer limited space for new music. The Christian charts are dominated by major label bands.

- Rock. Includes the subcategories of Active Rock (Linkin Park, Foo Fighters, Puddle of Mudd, Korn), Modern Rock (White Stripes), and Alternative (White Stripes, Red Hot Chili Peppers, Green Day). Many stations define the rock subcategories differently, and similar artists could appear on many different charts. This is the most difficult format to gain traction in.

- Urban. 300 stations. Ne-Yo, 50 Cent, Nelly, Kanye West, R. Kelly. This format is dominated by major labels.

- Classical. 150 stations. Primarily playing the "classics." Not much space for new music.

- Jazz. 150 stations. Two subcategories to this format: smooth jazz and traditional jazz. Traditional jazz offers some possibilities for the independent label/artist, but smooth jazz is more dominated by major label offerings.

- Spanish. 600 stations. Includes Latin Pop stations, Latin Rhythm, and others.

Charts and Reporting Commercial Radio Airplay

The results of a commercial radio campaign are currently reported in three main trade magazines: *FMQB*, *Radio & Records (R&R)*, and *Billboard*. Smaller commercial radio stations report their playlists to the trades in the same fashion as college radio reports to CMJ: manually through a fax or e-mail. Larger stations in major markets are monitored by either a company called BDS (that uses a computer to track airplay) or MediaBase (made up of humans that listen to the music played).

INDEPENDENT RADIO PROMOTERS

Similar to press, many stations in the radio industry rely upon independent promoters to present them with new music and provide them with the band's "story" (which, in the commercial radio world, typically includes other stations that have added the music). There are, however, some important differences between the work that press and radio indies do, and how they are paid for it.

At the college and noncommercial radio level, independent promoters forge personal relationships with the music directors and DJs, with the goal of convincing these gatekeepers to spin the records they are working. As we discussed earlier, noncommercial radio for the most part still plays music on its own merits and story. Indie promoters generally focus on specific genres of music and specialty shows, like blues, jazz, local music, and college radio. While it's more difficult for these indies to maintain long-standing relationships with college radio (for the fact that the staff continually rotates due to graduation), good indies definitely have access and relationships with specialty show hosts that labels and independent artists do not.

Independent promoters working Triple A and Americana commercial radio are also cut from the same cloth as noncommercial indies. These folks have years of relationships with their stations, and the good promoters work hard to present your music and your story in the best possible light. Of course, in the same way that publicists cannot guarantee print visibility, legit radio indies cannot guarantee spins. Their job is to get the music directors to hear the music, understand the background story, and help them to make an informed decision about whether or not the station should add the record into rotation.

Things start to get a bit more convoluted with the role of the independent promoter in the major market massive-reach stations. Whereas indie promoters who work noncommercial or Triple A radio typically get paid a fee for the entire campaign, it is not uncommon for indie promoters working large-scale commercial stations to get paid *per station* that adds the record. On the low end, an indie will get paid $1,000 per ad, and on the high end, this figure could reach upwards of $8,000! This is in addition to their regular campaign fee and other backroom shenanigans that are common in the highly competitive world of commercial radio.

So what is an independent artist to do for independent promotion? First, understand that a national commercial radio campaign spearheaded by an indie promoter is only a possibility (Triple A and Americana aside) if you have a several-hundred-thousand-dollar budget. Second, if your music fits into any of the formats that are more open to independent music (college, specialty shows, Triple A, Americana), a dedicated indie with station relationships and a good track record can definitely help you get wider exposure.

If you do decide to hire an independent promoter to work college radio, noncommercial radio, Triple A, or Americana, keep the following in mind.

What You Need to Look for in an Independent Radio Promoter

There are some shadowy figures in the music industry that might not always be completely honest and upfront about what they can do, how much they charge, and how hard they will work for you. The best independent promoters will likely not jump at the chance to work with you right away. Instead, they'll ask questions designed to determine if you are at the right stage in your career for a radio campaign, and they'll listen to your music to see if they can articulate it properly. There's no problem finding promo indies that are eager for your money. Many of them will try to blind you with what they can do and how many stations they can get behind your record without even asking a thing about your music or your long-term goals. Just like in the press world, the best indie promoters have relationships with stations, who expect that these promoters will bring them quality music with a good story. These folks will not take on your music if they feel it will diminish their relationships with their stations.

It's also important to determine how many projects your indie is currently working. If they're currently working a higher-profile project that is very similar to yours, it's likely that your release will not be worked with the same intensity.

Lastly, reputation is king. A great first step is to talk to other artists, labels, and managers about their experience and who they used. If you are looking to hire an indie college radio promoter, it also doesn't hurt to contact the indie promoters that CMJ itself recommends. CMJ list their Promoters of the Year on their site as part of their annual College Radio Award Nominees.

What an Indie Promoter Can (and Should) Do for You

For independent artists, the role of the indie promoter is to "quarterback" your entire radio campaign. What this means is that the promoter works to:

- Determine what stations make sense based on your goal, tour plans, and other marketing you have in place.

- Mail out your package (or instruct you on where to mail out the package). Your mailing should contain a full-length promo copy of your record or EP if you are going for noncommercial radio, or a single if you are going for commercial radio.

- Hit the phones! Follow up with all stations that have been sent your music. The promoter is finding out who received the CD, setting the stage with your band's story, determining interest, and asking if they will add the record to their rotation. This is the most important job of the indie promoter. Music directors get a ton of music, and these calls are designed to get your music out from the stack and listened to.

- If the promoter is working commercial radio, the promoter is not only working to get stations to add the record, but also working the stations to increase the amount of "spins" (plays) the record is getting. The higher the spins, the higher you will be on the commercial radio charts.

- Reporting. Good independent promoters will report their activities in weekly status reports notating the comments from the music or program directors. Typically, you will see comments like "Added," "Pass," "Hasn't listened to it yet," and "In rotation."

How Long You Should Hire an Indie Promoter For

Noncommercial campaigns typically last about eight to ten weeks. Commercial campaigns can last longer, depending on the results of the campaign.

INTERNET RADIO: THE FUTURE OF RADIO

"In my end is my beginning."
—T.S. Eliot, "East Coker"

Terrestrial commercial radio was an effective outlet for exposing new music to listeners in the 1960s and early 1970s under the freeform "AOR" (Album Oriented Rock) format. Under this format, DJs had the freedom to play long sets of music across many different genres of music. The songs played were not determined by the promotional efforts of labels, and DJs had the opportunity to play more adventurous and obscure tracks from both independent and major artists. As the format picked up, new listeners and advertising rates became more of a priority to station owners, and the programming slowly tightened up, eventually contributing to the lack of diversity problems we see today at commercial terrestrial radio.

The "end" has certainly been reached in terms of terrestrial commercial radio exposing consumers to new music on the sort of scale that was common in rock radio's heyday. But over the past five years, Internet radio has emerged as a vehicle that could possibly be the "new beginning" of radio promotion, with the ability to expose a huge amount of new music to consumers in the same fashion as free-form radio did forty years ago.

According to Edison Media Research, the weekly online radio audience increased from 11 percent to 13 percent of all Americans in 2008. In 2008, 33 million people listened to Internet radio every week, compared with 279 million terrestrial radio listeners. Although the current reach of satellite and Internet radio is far less than terrestrial radio, it's clear that the growth potential in nonterrestrial radio is huge. There's little doubt that nonterrestrial radio will continue to develop as an effective medium for exposing people around the world to new music. And the best part is that many of these outlets are very friendly to independent artists and labels.

Internet Radio and Social Networking

There are currently thousands of online radio stations, covering everything you can imagine listening to. Many of the best online radio stations can be found using aggregators like iTunes Radio or Yahoo Music, each of which lists hundreds of stations. For folks that are looking for a DJ to introduce them to new music and provide meaningful commercial-free dialogue on their particular musical interests, this brand of DJ-driven online radio hits the spot.

In addition to these DJ-driven online stations, a number of other online radio outlets have popped up that take advantage of music technology and social networking to provide listeners with a more personalized approach to music selection. Sites such as Pandora analyze the details of thousands of songs to find the common musical attributes these songs share. Users enter the names of their favorite artists, and Pandora scans their music database to create a playlist of similar songs that are personalized to each person's taste. Other online recommendation-based radio options include Last.fm (now owned by CBS), which has a heavier lean toward online community. Last.fm profiles each of their users' musical tastes, and the site's numerous social networking features recommend and play music based on the listening habits of other like-minded members of the community.

Edison Media Research also reported that in 2008, 41 percent of weekly online radio listeners have a profile on a social networking site. Getting your music played on an online radio station can have far-reaching effects for nurturing an online fan base as well!

Marketing to Internet Radio

We're still in the early days with online radio, and there's currently no standardized way to market and submit your music to online radio stations. You can add your music to some of the largest, like Pandora, through downloading and mailing in their Independent Music Submission Agreement (found on their site) along with your CD and bio. Last.fm is another friendly outlet for independent musicians. Other artist-friendly options include SongVault.fm. Billing itself as the "largest radio network for independent artists," the site provides an easy way for artists to upload their music as well as promote it with customizable HTML banner templates. Other online stations, like FineTune, simply do not take submissions from independent artists, and work with online distributors like CD Baby and The Orchard to get new music. Smaller online radio outlets need to be pitched in the same way you would pitch a blog—reaching the person that runs it, striking up a conversation with them, and asking for them to consider your music for placement onto their station. Much easier than working terrestrial radio!

Satellite Radio

In addition to online options, the other version of nonterrestrial radio is satellite radio. As of this writing, there are still two major players: XM Satellite Radio and SIRIUS Satellite Radio. However, merger plans were approved by the FCC in the middle of 2008. Together, XM and Sirius have more than 140 stations of music programming (including an amazing *Theme Time Radio Hour* with host Bob Dylan on XM). The benefits of satellite radio to consumers are many: less commercials, more programming, and more freedom within that programming. However, in terms of independent artist and label promotion, satellite radio does not have an open-door policy like many of the smaller and midsize online stations. Promoting your music to satellite radio takes connections within the organizations—connections that an independent artist likely does not have. If you want your music added to satellite radio, it's best to work with an independent promoter who has these personal connections.

INTERVIEW: BOB JAMIESON,
FORMER CEO OF RCA/BMG

*Bob Jamieson is the former CEO of RCA Music Group, BMG
North America, and is a respected leader in the music industry
with over thirty years of experience both in the U.S. and abroad.*

Where do you see radio headed?

I hope traditional radio gets back to playing more music and
exposing the listeners to more great artists, not just pop and
hip-hop hits. People will continue to pick up and enjoy satellite radio, as long as they can keep it operating with little or no
advertising, which I hope will continue to happen. There is a lot
more variety, and the public really doesn't like all those commercials. Hopefully satellite radio will force commercial radio to open
up their playlists, and perhaps some stations will begin to play
what we used to call AOR radio, which is free-form radio. That's
where you used to be able to hear a lot of the new artists that you
would not hear on the Top 40. What I think is going to happen in
the future is that someone like Clear Channel, a company that
owns four or five stations in a single market (and 1,200 across
the country), may take one of their smaller-rated stations and
try it as a free-form. I think it would win for the business, and it
would win for the public.

Summary

There's no question that working a record to radio is an expensive and difficult process, particularly with commercial radio,
where the playlists are tight and the majors dominate the field.
That being said, there are a number of radio opportunities available for developing artists outside of mainstream commercial
stations. It's crucial for artists to realize that national terrestrial
radio promotion is an activity that should take place once a
solid community is in place. While the barrier for online radio is
relatively low, both in costs and effort, promotion to terrestrial
stations is a different story. It's essential that before you engage
in the expense of radio promotion, you have the infrastructure to
take advantage of any play that you do receive.

The radio world is in tremendous upheaval (like much of the
music industry). Expect some major changes ahead in this area
as labels diversify their interests from their current record-sales-
based model (which for the majors relies heavily on commercial
radio exposure).

Workshop

> Research the radio stations in your local area. Based on what was discussed in this chapter, outline what options exist for developing artists (specialty shows, noncommercial radio outlets, college stations) and what kind of artist promotions are these stations doing. If you are (or are involved with) an active artist, what radio format would you pursue for your own music, and when would you pursue it? Do you see non-terrestrial radio as a valid marketing option for artists?

10 | Making the Most of a Tour

Over and above the obvious perks of being on the road—getting to really know your bandmates, eating at the same chain fast food restaurant twice in one day, etc.—touring is instrumental in bringing your act to the next level. Now, what this next level means is entirely up to you. For some, it means playing your songs at local coffee shops and pubs to a local crowd. For artists that are a bit more ambitious, a national tour provides the "spark" that will kick-start your sales and marketing machine—if you have a plan and stay on top of the fundamentals.

Touring is your chance to show everyone what you can do, and it's essential that you lay it all down at every gig. Nothing helps to build a devoted fan base quicker than an absolutely amazing live show. People want to see and hear you do something that they can't do. The best bandleaders were legendary for choosing musicians that absolutely blew the crowd away. James Brown, Buddy Rich, and Frank Zappa all perfectly understood the importance of converting potential at their shows into evangelists for their music by performing fantastic live events.

Consider the following:

- Income from CD sales continue to fall: 48 percent of teenagers did not buy a single CD in 2007! (Source: The NPD Group)

- Total primary-market concert ticket sales climbed to a record $3.9 billion in 2007, up 8 percent from $3.6 billion in 2006 and representing the ninth consecutive year that combined concert grosses in the U.S. and Canada have hit an all-time high. (Source: Pollstar)

- Record labels are aggressively pursuing "360" contracts, which give them a percentage of merch and touring revenue.

- Major acts such as Prince, Radiohead, and Nine Inch Nails are using their recorded music as a promotional vehicle to sell tickets to their stadium shows.

The impact a successful touring plan has on marketing and a band's revenue stream cannot be understated.

KEY PLAYERS IN THE TOURING BUSINESS

Like any other part of the music business, there are several gate-keepers involved in the touring industry that you'll need to work with in order to schedule, book, promote, and perform live events. In the beginning stage of any band's career, many of these tasks are done by the band members. As a band progresses and builds its career, there are some gigs that are better left to the professionals. In the touring industry, these are the friendly faces you are going to want to have on your side:

Tour Manager

The tour manager's main responsibilities sound easy: be organized, and get the band from point A to point B with the least amount of trouble. But in practice, the role of the tour manager can be incredibly stressful. For artists that are early on in their career and playing smaller club dates, the tour manager is responsible for getting the band to its destination city on time, getting the band to its sound check on time, and getting the band to any interviews, signings, or retail appearances on time. Not an easy task, especially when you are working with creative types that might not be focused on punctuality. The tour manager is also in constant contact with the artist's personal manager to keep the tour rolling smoothly. Also, in the band's early career, the tour manager is responsible for settling up with the club after the night's gig, and for budgeting responsibilities (per diems for band members, etc.) as well.

For artists that are playing larger venues, the tour manager's job expands to include a number of other responsibilities. Working with the personal manager, the tour manager will work to hire the road crew that will support the tour. They'll subcontract the lighting companies, sound companies, and the trucking and bussing companies. (We're talking big tours, here.) They also work to create, and enforce, the *contract rider* (the document that provides the clubs with details on stage design, proper sound systems and lighting configurations, as well as an artist's personal requests like meals and backstage accommodations) and itineraries specific for the tour. For a wonderful collection of tour riders (outlining some bizarre requests, from prune juice to aromatherapy candles), visit www.thesmokinggun.com/backstagetour.

Booking Agent

It's completely possible (and preferable) for artists to book their own shows when they are starting out. Booking yourself is good for a couple of reasons. First, it is helpful to understand how the touring business operates. Perhaps more important, it saves developing artists money, which can be better spent creating merch to sell or on other community-building activities. Providing a percentage of one's income to an agent in the early stages of a career wouldn't make sense for the artist, and plus, the income that you might get from playing in smaller clubs is not enough to warrant the time and energy of a booking agent. Similar to physical distribution, when you are no longer able to handle the work yourself, it makes sense to bring in a professional.

Booking agents are in high demand. Artists are tuned into the fact that royalty sales from records are not paying the bills, and many more artists are turning to heavier touring schedules as their primary source of income. The role of the booking agent is to work with a manager to help route an artist's tour, determine what particular venues the artist will play, and work with the promoter to figure out how much the artist will get paid. Booking agents have a wealth of contacts both at the venue level and within the rest of the industry that they use to help artists secure opening slots with larger artists, secure corporate sponsorships, and undertake other work on the artist's behalf. The largest booking agencies (like the William Morris Agency, Monterey Peninsula Artists, and Ted Kurland Associates) have employees that are specialists in different territories across the U.S. Booking agents work on a commission basis, and typically earn 10 percent of an artist's performance guarantees (an agreed minimum amount that an artist can expect to receive at any given performance).

What an agent looks for in an artist:

- a draw in multiple states

- a personal manager

- additional support: press buzz, great story, radio/retail support, previous high profile gigs

Before jumping in with a booking agent, be sure you are really ready for one. Booking agents work on a commission basis and could represent dozens of artists. If the booking agent sees that there is not much interest in your band, he or she will likely focus on someone else that is producing income for them. The last thing developing artists want is to have their tours booked by people who are not dedicated to their cause!

INTERVIEW: DAN PERAINO, BOOKING AGENT

Booker T. & the MG's Dan Peraino has worked with Boston's Concerted Efforts agency for ten years. Concerted Efforts works with artists as diverse as Booker T. & the MG's, Marc Ribot, Jill Sobule, and Juliana Hatfield.

What are booking agents looking for when deciding which artists to work with?

From my standpoint, an agent should be a fan of the artists they work with, both their music and their live show. Also important is a proactive manager who really knows how to manage an artist. A major record label is not as important these days, but some kind of marketing support is still better than a DIY release. It's more difficult to develop unsigned artists unless they already have a fan base in other markets. We usually have a few unsigned artists we strongly believe will develop and grow.

How hard is it for artists to get a booking agent now?

I think it's really difficult to get an established agent these days. MySpace and the Internet have been instrumental in increasing the amount of touring artists, but there are only so many agents. There is also more risk and investment for agents these days with the absence of label support and general competition for the fan base. Remember, there are only so many rock clubs in Omaha, NE and Columbus, OH. Agents seem to be booking further in advance—up to eighteen months—because there are so many artists filling the venues.

How do you find new bands to work with? Do you listen to unsolicited packages from bands? Do you get info from managers or labels?

We mostly get info from labels, publicists, managers, even artists themselves. I don't generally accept unsolicited packages. Sending a Web link for streaming audio is best. If I have time to check it out, I'll probably respond, if I like it.

What is a typical fee an artist might pay a booking agent?

The standard fee is 10 percent. If the agency is also doing management work, or help with advancing, record deals, travel logistics, etc., the fee could increase from there.

What kind of offers are you seeing from promoters and club bookers currently?

Depending on the artist and venue, it really runs the gamut. It could be a straight door deal with 80 percent of gross gate receipts from dollar one, to guarantees in the tens of thousands plus a percentage of profits after promoter expenses.

How has the Internet changed how your section of the music industry operates?

The Internet has helped our artists connect with their fans, other artists, and other artists' fans all over the world, which in turn helps increase their fan base and sell tickets. This also allows the artist and/or record label to market their products more efficiently.

How do you find appropriate opening acts for bands? What characteristics are you looking for when you match headlining and opening acts?

Agents correspond with each other and share routing to see where it might be beneficial to put certain artists together. Sometimes, it has to do with box office history in a specific market, and in other situations, the artists themselves might just want a creative bill. Pollstar, MySpace, venue Web sites, etc., are good search tools to see who might be crossing paths.

What are the top three things that artists can do to make the job of a booking agent easier?

(1) Get a manager (experienced). (2) Get a record label, specialized marketing team, and/or publicist who loves you. (3) Make friends with everyone you meet on tour, including other artists, promoters, venue staff, and audience.

Tour Accountant and Road Manager

At the highest echelons of the touring industry, the responsibilities of the tour manager are simply too great for a single person, and a more robust staff is required to handle various management tasks. A *tour accountant* has an intimate understanding of the particular deal that the booking agent and promoter have worked out, and is responsible for settling the show at the end of the night. The accountant is responsible for doling out petty cash and per diems, and adhering to a previously determined budget so the band ends up in the black. A *road manager* takes on the scheduling duties and travel plans, and the production and stage managers take care of the technical and onstage requirements such as load in and load out, starting the sound check, and all other incidentals required for a smooth show.

Club Owners, Promoters, Event Organizers

The other side of the coin is the folks that you will be working with that are not part of your intimate team:

Club Owners

Typically, small club owners act as their own promoters. Their primary concern is to draw people in to sell drinks. More often than not, they offer little in the way of up-front compensation for the band, as they are not interested in taking any sort of loss if the band is not successful.

Promoters

A promoter is a step up from a club owner. The promoter takes on much more risk than a club owner. Often, in order to secure a popular touring artist, a promoter provides a deal to a touring artist that includes a guarantee of a minimum payment, with a deposit in advance. The smaller regional promoters usually do not own their own club or venue, but instead work with third-party venues that are rented. However, some of the larger promoters (like Live Nation, which is the touring division of Clear Channel) are involved in several areas of the touring business, from ownership of the venues to ownership of the radio stations that promote the artists to the regional advertising outlets like highway billboards.

Event Organizers

Anyone coordinating live music at a particular time and destination is an event organizer. From a major mutual fund company hosting a party for their high-net-worth clients, to festivals like South by Southwest in Austin and CMJ in New York City, event organizers run the gamut from a more advanced understanding of the industry, to knowing nothing at all about deals, guarantees, and equipment.

Booking Your Gig

As we discussed previously, booking agents are an amazing resource for bands that are at the right level in their career. Booking gigs is a tedious, time-consuming process, and similar to press writers, the talent agents (club owners or people hired to find good bands for the clubs) at many of these venues are inundated with press kits, e-mails, and follow-up calls. However, unlike press writers, booking agents don't need (and in many cases don't want) a physical press kit from you. More and more often, venues these days are looking for electronic versions of the elements contained in the press kit: music, images, press quotes, bio, label, and distribution background—all things that prove that you can draw folks to their club. All of these elements can certainly be laid out in a well-designed Web site, perhaps on one page under "press info."

Additionally, over the past few years a company called Sonicbids has cornered the Electronic Press Kit (EPK) market. Sonicbids' trademarked EPK provides artists with an easy-to-update personal page on their site, which contains all the elements a talent agent looks for. Additionally, Sonicbids has exclusive relationships with festivals and clubs around the world, including Telluride Bluegrass Festival, NXNE (North by Northeast), NEMO (New England Music Organization), and hundreds more. Many of these festivals only take submissions through Sonicbids, as it streamlines their application process. It's still a good idea to have physical press kits available on the off chance that a venue prefers this, but it makes good sense to contact the venue (or visit their Web site) to find the preferred method of contact.

PROMOTING THE SHOW: WORKING WITH THE VENUE

Once the artist, manager, and booking agent (if applicable) have routed the tour, booked the dates, worked out the finances, and have the people you need in place, the next step is to promote the dates!

What a Venue *Might* Do for You

I use the term "might" here, because all venues have different degrees of promotional support. (And some venues have folks that are a bit less marketing-focused than others!) In the very least, venues of all sizes should:

- Put up posters, which you provide to them. Posters should be sized 11x17 (these fit easily into a #6 Jiffy mailer when folded). Depending on the venue, posters will usually be hung up in several spots. At Ryko, we usually assumed ten to fifteen posters per date. The promoters/talent buyers will usually tell you how many they could use. Any excess posters can be used at retail or with the street team.

- Add you to their itinerary of upcoming events. This likely will mean a tag in any advertising the venue does in the local daily/weekly, a mention on their calendar on their Web site, and a tag in any print calendars they do as well.

- Send an e-mail out to their list, announcing your upcoming show.

- Place a dedicated ad in the region's weekly entertainment publication with ticket and show information. (This is actually coordinated with the promoter, and in many cases is considered an expense that comes out of the artist's bottom line.)

- Some venues are also interested in a promo copy of your record to play between sets of other music, in their bar area, etc.

All of these things should be discussed with the folks at the venue as early as possible. It's in the best interest of the venue to support your gig in whatever way they can, but because of the quantity of artists and the high turnover at some of these outlets, anything you can do to help move the venue promotion process along will be appreciated.

PROMOTING THE SHOW: WHAT YOU SHOULD BE DOING TO PROMOTE YOURSELF

In tandem with squaring away the promotion that the venue will do on your behalf, artists should also mobilize their own resources and fan base to make individual shows as successful as possible. There is nothing more powerful than an artist's relationship with his or her own fans.

Considerations for Maximizing Your Fan Base while on Tour

Optimize Your Street/Viral Team. We've previously discussed the importance of a successful street team. All the hard work of finding evangelists for your music and creating ways to make them feel part of the band experience comes back to you when you have tour dates to market. A successful street team should be sent resources to help promote your live events. Posters, counter cards, or photocopied announcements tagging the venue, date, and time are a great start. Keep in mind that it's not legal to hang posters in public places. Your street team should focus on lifestyle outlets that fans of your band might frequent in their particular market. Bulletin boards at coffee shops and ice cream parlors, and window visibility in hip resale, apparel, or record shops (or wherever your fans tend to shop) should all be targeted. You might also want to connect with your street team rep in each tour market to see if there are any lifestyle outlets that might be interested in playing your music in-store. (It is possible!) Lastly, a cost-effective route for getting posters or one-sheets out to your street team is to offer a downloadable PDF on your site, which your team can print out and distribute.

Mailing List. Developing a mailing list should be at the top of your list of tour promotional strategies. Informing your fans about upcoming dates is a great way to get folks to come out to your gig. Timing is crucial. Send an announcement e-mail once you've booked your run of dates (if this is a national or regional tour), and follow up with geo-targeted messages (messages tailored to a specific zip code) talking about the dates in these possible areas closer to the show date. FanBridge is one e-mail campaign manager that allows for geo-targeting.

Splitting Promotional Responsibilities with Another Band

In your communications to your fans, tag (call out, or link to) any artists that you are playing with, and ask the same of these artists to their fan base. It's likely that any artists you're sharing the stage with have some common musical bond with you (unless the show is very poorly booked or purposefully eclectic). The fans of the other band on your bill might be more receptive to showing up early or staying later if your music is recommended by a band they trust.

Web Visibility

Once your tour is booked and confirmed, your tour dates should be front and center on your Web site. Make it clear in the news section that you are playing live, and provide links to the venues and ways to pay right from your site. The easier you can make it for your fans to know about your dates, the better.

PROMOTING THE SHOW: PRESS

Touring kick-starts all the other marketing segments that are important to an artist's overall success. This is particularly true when it comes to press. A good press campaign has two distinct parts:

1. **Pre-release press,** focused on raising awareness of an upcoming record in long-lead press outlets, lifestyle magazines, genre specific mags, major national pubs, and so on.

2. **Tour press,** which is primarily focused on geographic-specific markets' press outlets.

Touring provides an artist's publicist with the chance to re-approach some of the major dailies and weeklies who may have passed on covering the initial album release. Touring can also help build an artist's buzz from the bottom up (rather than the top-down approach of major national outlets) through coverage in the smaller weeklies and dailies that may not have been part of the initial major national record release campaign.

Ideally, tour press outlets should be serviced six weeks out from the date, and followed up on as the date nears.

Tour Press Release

A tour press release differs from a record-release press release in a couple ways. While the main purpose of an album press release is to introduce the band and create a story that will provoke the reader into listening to the music, the main function of a tour press release is to convey—as quickly and as succinctly as possible—that the band is on tour. A good tour press release includes:

- a short intro announcing the tour and tagging the existing record (if applicable)
- some sort of local angle, if possible
- a quote or description of the band's music
- a listing of the dates
- a footer containing the contact info of the publicist, as well as a leading statement about action items, such as "To schedule an interview or review this show, please contact xxx..."

What You Should Be Looking for from Tour Press

There are three tangible goals of tour press outreach:

Previews. Previews are designed to help drive folks to the show.

Reviews. Concert reviews provide a great resource in raising the visibility of your band in specific markets, and can have a tangible effect on sales (if they are positive!).

Interviews. Interviews are a step up from both previews and reviews. An interview with press allows the band's personality to shine and lets readers know, in the artists' own words, why someone should check their band out. Interviews typically run with a photo, which again helps to bridge the gap between the fans and the band. Interviews happen either (a) the day of the show in person at the venue, or (b) with "phoners" (phone interviews) done prior to the band entering the market.

Other Considerations

> A publicist working tour press will need specific info on the dates: time, other artists sharing the bill, if the venue is 21+, etc. Publicists (also radio promo and retail folks) also need the ability to provide a certain number of tickets to VIPs (primarily writers). If a band is on a label, the label usually foots the bill for ticket buys. Additionally, an amount of tickets is sometimes worked into the tour rider for bigger name artists. Lastly, for artists in the beginning stages of their careers, these VIP ticket requests can come out of the band's salary for the night! No one ever said it was easy to get into the music business!

PROMOTING THE SHOW: RETAIL

> Similar to press, touring provides a reason for retail to take interest in you, whether you have a distribution deal or not. Retailers understand that an incredible live show, coupled with press and radio visibility, creates a viral effect: folks are talking about the show, reading the press, hearing the music, and if they are so inclined, will want to buy the record.

Promoting Your Show and Selling Your CDs

> As we learned in chapter 5, independent stores are a whole lot more supportive of artists than the big box retailers. There is more space available for promo items, there is more opportunity for in-store play, and for artists without a national distribution deal, many independent record stores will buy in some records on consignment if they know you are playing in the area (especially if you have press and radio support!).

> Key points when marketing to retail around a tour:

> - If you do not have a national distribution deal, it makes sense to identify and approach the key indies in each market and inquire about their consignment policies. Every store is different, but before any retailer will do any sort of marketing for you, you'll need to have your CD in their stores. Normal buy-in is one or two pieces. However, once you've developed this relationship with the retailer and sold these pieces, it's much easier to approach them the next time you are in the area to take in additional units.

PRESS RELEASE FOR JON FISHMAN'S PORK TORNADO TOUR

The main purpose of this press release was to support Phish drummer Jon Fishman's Pork Tornado tour. The release also tags Pork Tornado's recent record, which the band was touring behind, but the headline and detail in this release was principally designed to get folks out to the show.

SERIOUS TORNADO ADVISORY
PORK TORNADO EMBARKS ON NATIONAL TOUR

Rykodisc is pleased to announce the release of the self-titled debut from Pork Tornado, a band led by Jon Fishman, the drummer for the inimitable band Phish. The album was produced by Jon and Dan Archer, features studio versions of many classics from their live repertoire, and manages to plant its hind quarters all over the genre map, from traditional country and bar blues to raucous funk to more experimental explorations.

"It's a freak show," says Fishman, on the band he cofounded five years ago. "It's the funniest thing. It's just the weirdest...."

For once, the garrulous percussionist is lost for words. Well, just how exactly does one explain Pork Tornado? Try to imagine a giant cyclonic inferno sweeping across the musical landscape, sucking up and then regurgitating some unholy combination of Frank Zappa and the Mothers of Invention, James Brown, and the Fabulous Flames, and Bob Wills and the Texas Playboys.

Pork Tornado sweeps across the country for twenty-nine shows in October and November:

10/9	Pearl Street	Northampton	MA
10/10	Paradise	Boston	MA
10/11	Lupo's	Providence	RI
10/12	Bowery Ballroom	New York	NY
10/13	Theater of Living Arts	Philadelphia	PA
10/14	Water Street Music Hall	Rochester	NY
10/16	Odeon	Cleveland	OH
10/17	Bogart's	Cincinnati	OH
10/18	Blind Pig	Ann Arbor	MI
10/19	Double Door	Chicago	IL
10/21	First Avenue	Minneapolis	MN
10/23	Mississippi Nights	St. Louis	MO
10/24	Blue Note	Columbia	MO

10/25	Bottleneck	Lawrence	KS
10/26	Fox Theatre	Boulder	CO
10/28	Harry O's	Park City	UT
10/30	Showbox	Seattle	WA
10/31	Roseland	Portland	OR
11/1	Slim's	San Francisco	CA
11/2	Roxy	Los Angeles	CA
11/3	House of Blues	Las Vegas	NV
11/6	Trees	Dallas	TX
11/7	La Zona Rosa	Austin	TX
11/8	Tipitina's	New Orleans	LA
11/9	Variety Playhouse	Atlanta	GA
11/10	The Orange Peel	Asheville	NC
11/12	Starr Hill Music Hall	Charlottesville	VA
11/13	9:30 Club	Washington	DC
11/14	Northern Lights	Albany	NY

For more information regarding tour and ticketing please visit
www.porktornado.com

For publicity information or to book an interview, please contact Mike King at
Rykodisc [phone number, e-mail address].

- Once your CD is in the stores (through consignment or regular distribution channels), a forward-thinking retailer might want some of the same promo pieces that you use for record retail marketing: 11x17 posters (tagging date and performance venue), a copy of the record for in-store play (white-label burned copy is fine), and possibly a bin card (to help locate the disc). Amazing retailers might also give you preferential visibility to help connect the dots between the tour and the CD in their store.

- If your band is hot, the retailer might also want you to perform an in-store with them. In-stores are always a good way to help move existing product, and may also increase the retailer's buy-in. However, it's important not to kill the momentum of your show. If you are doing an in-store the same day as your show, a good idea is to try something outside of what you will be doing at the venue. A rock band might want to try an "exclusive acoustic" event, for example. This way, your fans will feel like they are getting something special rather than seeing exactly what they will be seeing later in the evening.

If you are signed to a label:

- A wise label will follow the tour closely, and adjust co-op spends where it makes sense. Co-op opportunities vary from store to store, but could include endcap or listening post visibility with a tag to the tour date, a co-op ad in the local weekly, or daily tagging the date, special sale pricing, etc.

- The director of sales at a label might be interested in bringing the store buyer out to the show if they are a big fan of your music, with the hopes that they will buy in more product or give you preferred visibility in store.

- Occasionally, a retail chain would be interested in hosting a band at the corporate headquarters for a meet and greet and to perform an acoustic set at lunch.

TOUR SUPPORT FROM A LABEL

There's no question that touring makes a huge difference in raising an artist's visibility and selling music on a regional basis. However, touring is hard work. The drive times can be long, artists tend to have to travel in cramped confined places (which can cause irritability), and some of the folks involved in the touring industry are not a picture of politeness and honesty. Additionally, when you are trying to make inroads in particular markets that you have not visited before, there's a chance that you might actually lose money by playing the date (low turnout, low merch sales). And unless you have a bio diesel tour bus like Willie Nelson, high gas prices are going to be a major cost you need to figure into your budget, as well.

Labels, of course, understand the importance of sending their artists on tour. They know that it's in their best interest to have their artists on the road for as long as possible. They also understand that for developing artists, the income sometimes does not cover the expenses. Tour support is a recoupable marketing expense that labels will undertake if they feel it is important to the success of the tour, and has a positive effect on record sales.

How Tour Support Works

The label does not just freely give out tour support when an artist asks for it. While tour support may be in an artist's contract, the artist or manager needs to present a detailed explanation of dates, expected income, and costs associated with playing these dates, including:

- fuel costs

- per diem (food allowance) for band members

- lodging

- miscellaneous

The label takes a look at the expected costs and income, and in most cases, debates some of the costs with the manager. A figure is usually decided on (which is called the tour shortfall), and the label cuts a check for the difference. Once the tour is complete, the label expects proper accountings (receipts for expenses, income from ticket and merch sales) from the manager. Again, tour support is recoupable from an artist's royalties. For a developing artist, it makes sense to try to make your tour as self-sustaining as possible (staying at friends' houses, for example). It's no fun to be deep in the red at the end of a tour, especially if your records are cross-collateralized.

Routing Your Tour

Touring the east coast is easy; all the major markets are within an easy day's drive from one another. The Midwest and West Coast are another story. When routing your tour, pay close attention to distances and the expected income/promotional exposure you will likely get by playing out-of-the-way venues. Barstow, CA might seem like a cool place when you pass it on your way to Las Vegas from Los Angeles, but does it really make sense to play there?

 SPOTLIGHT: BRANDON BUSH FROM
SUGARLAND AND TRAIN ON
THE IMPORTANCE OF TOURING:

"In the past fives years as a member of Train, and more recently as a touring member of Sugarland, I've had a really unique perspective. I've seen a rock band that can do well, make its bread and butter on the road, but has a series of radio hits that really defines the band and propels it forward. It's interesting to leave that world, where I am a band member and am intensely interested in all aspects of the business, to come out here to tour with Sugarland as an employee where I've got one focus: to show up and put on a great show. The touring income in country music is incredible—it's very healthy. Sugarland is filling seats and people are loving it. Last summer, we were opening for Kenny Chesney, and he plays stadiums. Here, we're playing to 60,000 people who

are buying tickets and coming to see a show. It's clear that touring is the income for a working band. That is the focus. The business has changed. Whether you're on a label that has its own struggles and are trying to figure out how to translate record sales into money, or you're off a label and you're trying to figure out how to distribute music in a way that gets to people and is an income stream, it's not easy. Those are challenges, where touring is what touring was ten years ago. It's entertaining people; it's putting on a good show. And I think I've seen that more in country music than rock. Touring is firm, strong, and it is what you focus on."

Summary

As mechanical royalties from CD sales drop, artists are increasingly looking for alternative revenue sources. Touring is absolutely essential to the overall financial health and longevity of every artist. There is certainly more competition than ever before in the segment. However, a well-run tour provides artists with not only financial benefits, but also invigorates all the other marketing segments to provide artists with maximum overall visibility.

Workshop

Create a dream outline for a ten-day national tour. (We'll take this back to reality when we talk about budgeting in the next chapter!) Be sure to cover the following areas:

1. What venues will you be playing, and how will you advance these dates?

2. What prominent retail outlets exist in these areas?

3. What radio stations will you target in advance of your date?

4. What local press outlets will you work with to support these dates?

5. What is the most effective way to mobilize a ten-person street team in these areas (what lifestyle outlets would be appropriate)?

6. Describe options for mobilizing your online fans.

PART THREE

Putting It All Together

11 Timing Is Everything!

Throughout this book, we've looked at the broad marketing segments and tools that marketers have at their disposal. But just like a good comedy routine or stock sales, pulling off an effective marketing campaign is all about timing. What good is it to have all these tools and techniques in your kit without knowing when to use them? A common theme that we've talked about is that nothing happens in a vacuum. In this chapter, we'll talk about how to properly roll out your pre-release marketing plan, what to do when the music is out, and what goes into developing your phase II marketing plan.

TIMING THE PRE-RELEASE MARKETING OF YOUR RECORD

Artists should always be thinking about marketing, whether they have a new release on the horizon or not. Community-building activities such as adding to your e-mail list, optimizing your Web site, and performing live events are essential to the well-being of a band at every stage in its career. Continuing to organize a fan base will pay big dividends when you do plan on releasing some music or putting together a tour.

Over and above these general evergreen marketing initiatives, there are a number of specific items a band needs to consider and execute prior to releasing a record. All of these efforts build on the successful execution of the previous effort, so you can quickly see how labels and independent musicians that are disorganized can fall behind. But if you stay on top of a defined timeline, it's not difficult to pull off a record release with the proper marketing support on the date that you originally planned.

As with most endeavors, the more planning that goes into a project, the more successful that project is going to be. Let's take an in-depth look at the components that need to be addressed prior to the release of a new record.

Street Date

All pre-release marketing efforts are timed off of this date, and in a perfect world, all your marketing efforts will be planned to have the maximum effect on this date as well. Record labels set a particular project's street date for both revenue reasons (just like any other company or individual, a label wants to generate relatively consistent income throughout the year) as well as maximum impact. For example, major labels routinely set the street date of major releases to hit during the holiday season, when many people purchase music for gifts. For an independent band, street date can be a little more arbitrary. Independents might be wise to avoid a holiday street date, as the promotional outlets will be jammed with more highly funded releases, but otherwise, choosing a street date is up to you. It's not uncommon for artists to plan their street date to coincide with a major festival date or industry event like South by Southwest or CMJ.

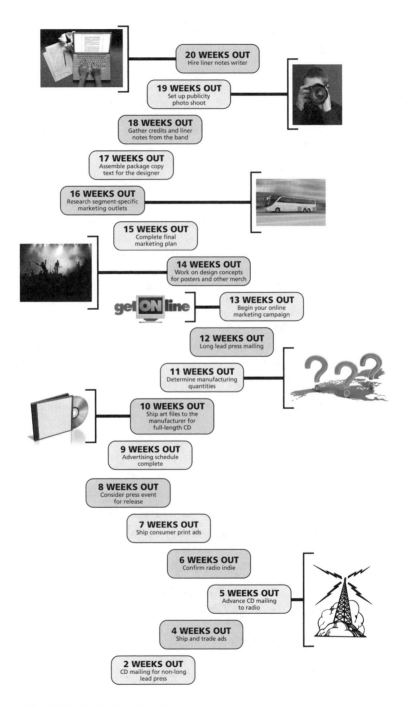

Fig. 11.1. Marketing Plan Timeline

LONG LEAD PRE-RELEASE MARKETING
(15 TO 20 WEEKS OUT FROM STREET DATE)

A well-executed marketing plan begins far in advance of the record's street date. Rykodisc was pretty good at sticking to a predetermined street date. (Blowing a street date costs time and money, and independent labels don't have much of either!) Part of this was due to the fact that we planned new releases twenty weeks in advance. A number of these far-out elements in the timeline were internal related items (notifying the U.K. office of the release, confirming the publishing with our satellite publishing office, etc.). The following core marketing elements are ideally put into action 15 to 20 weeks out from street date.

Budgeting, goals, and planning. Before you move forward with engaging in any pre-release planning or marketing, it's necessary to have an idea of the budget and a unified idea of the goals for the project (the elements we discussed in chapter 1). All the "minor details" of the rest of the marketing plan stem from the overall goal of the project. Here are some of the overall planning activities one needs to consider, and the dates they need to be considered:

- 20 weeks out from street date: Your budgeting plan should be ready.

- 18 weeks out: Confirm the list price of the release.

- 17 weeks out: Draft an overview marketing plan of the record.

- 16 weeks out: Research specific marketing/budget ideas in regards to sales, radio, press, touring, Internet, and promo materials.

- 15 weeks out: Complete your final marketing plan.

- 15 weeks out: Finalize your Sales/Distribution sheet draft.

Packaging elements. There's a whole lot more than just cover art that goes into an effective package. Liner notes are another way for a band to create an emotional connection with their fans. And although the trend is definitely towards digital music, there's no doubt that the lack of liner notes and cover art with some online releases is being addressed as we speak. The full packaging elements of a fan-friendly release should be considered and addressed several months out from street date. These elements include:

- 20 weeks out from street date: Hire a liner-note writer (if necessary).

- 19 weeks out: Execute a publicity shoot (for cover images, as well as press-only images).

- 18 weeks out: Gather liner notes and credits from the band.

- 17 weeks out: Assemble the package copy text document for the designer (includes legal and publishing info).

- 17 weeks out: Edit liner notes copy (if necessary).

- 16 weeks out: Start a designer on package design, ads, posters, Web, etc.

- 15 weeks out: Create sales-focused copy for the underside of spine cap (obi).

Promotional materials/activities. Once you've determined the scope, reach, goals, and budget of your project, the next step is putting the necessary promotional elements into production. Some of these items might include:

- 16 weeks out from street date: Select/confirm track for commercial radio (if applicable).

- 15 weeks out: Select/confirm exclusive Internet-only track.

- 15 weeks out: Make advances for key press, distribution, and internal use (street team members or possible publicity/radio indies).

MODERATE LEAD PRE-RELEASE MARKETING (7 TO 14 WEEKS OUT FROM STREET DATE)

Once the stage is set and you have your package, plan, and promotional ideas in place, the next step is to focus on the more specific elements and defined segments of your pre-release marketing campaign.

Pre-release marketing. The major marketing segments all have varying time requirements that marketers have to adhere to in order to effectively support a street date. Considerations should include:

- 14 weeks out from street date: Create a distribution ad (for physical distribution catalog, if applicable).

- 13 weeks out: Finalize your press release.

- 13 weeks out: Confirm an independent publicist (if applicable).

- 13 weeks out: Begin your Web campaign: Updating site with new release info, press release, album image, music, etc.

- 12 weeks out: Publicity advance mailing to long lead press contacts.
- 12 weeks out: Create your print advertising schedule.
- 12 weeks out: Write advertising copy.
- 11 weeks out: Create and send out distribution sheets to distribution reps (if applicable).
- 10 weeks out: Finalize tour plans (if signed to a label, discuss tour support options).
- 8 weeks out: Begin to think about a press event (if applicable).
- 7 weeks out: Consumer print ads begin to ship to longer lead pubs.

Packaging/merch elements.

Begin working on design concepts for posters, P.O.P. materials, ads:

- 14 weeks out from street date: Begin working on design concepts for posters, P.O.P. materials, ads.
- 14 weeks out: Approve cover image.
- 11 weeks out: Decide on manufacturing quantities.
- 10 weeks out: Ship art files to the manufacturer for full-length CD and commercial single (if applicable).

SHORT LEAD PRE-RELEASE MARKETING (UP TO 6 WEEKS OUT)

At six weeks out, most of the details and overview plans should have been put in place, and the final weeks leading up to street date consist of seeing these plans through and tying all the pieces together. Things that should be considered in the last few weeks prior to street date include:

Pre-release marketing.

- 6 weeks out from street date: Confirm a radio indie (if applicable).
- 5 weeks out: Coordinate co-op ad materials for retail (copy, cover art, marketing details).
- 5 weeks out: Send out advance mailing to radio.
- 4 weeks out: Ship trade ad.
- 2 weeks out: Send commercial CD radio and tour press mailings.

Packaging/merch elements.

- 5 weeks out from street date: Posters/collateral due from the printer.

HOW TO SERVICE KEY MARKETING OUTLETS PRE-RELEASE

The pre-release marketing process is in flux. The recent trend of selling a digital version of a record weeks (or days) after getting the master back from the studio is a way for more established artists to add an additional layer of Internet-based marketing support to the traditional press, radio, retail, and distribution segments. Artists who've released their music digitally without any other traditional marketing support are able to build up an online buzz, which accomplishes three things:

- Online buzz gets their hardcore fans their music as soon as it is available.

- Word of mouth/blog marketing helps with sales of the physical record, as well as concert ticket sales.

- It also provides a base of income that can be used to purchase more traditional marketing visibility when the physical product is released.

All this being said, releasing a record digitally without any pre-release marketing support is most effective for artists that have previously spent the time and marketing dollars to attract and build up their fan bases. And even if a band releases its record immediately following its completion, a full marketing campaign should still follow. If no one is aware that you exist, it's pretty hard to sell your music, digital or otherwise.

The key marketing segments that all bands (both established and developing bands) need to consider prior to the release of their record are serviced at different points (with different items) throughout the pre-release marketing campaign. Let's look at the needs of the individual marketing segments.

Pre-Release Marketing to Press

Publicity can require the longest lead time in your pre-release marketing campaign, depending on your target outlets. Some major national publications work several months in advance, and writers still tend to want physical pieces to review (rather than digital files). Rather than bumping up the production date of the final physical product, music marketers typically make and send out advance copies of the record for press review. Advances are produced in the following fashion:

- No booklet insert
- Contact info in the tray card, with publicity contact info first
- Release date prominent throughout
- Promotional blurb on the rear of the tray card
- Track listing
- Publishing and legal lines
- "For Promotional Use Only" legal copy

Pre-Release Marketing to Radio

Unlike publicity, radio has a very short lead time. Most radio campaigns begin only several weeks out from street date, to produce the most visibility as close to street date as possible. There are two ways to service radio outlets' pre-release of your record.

Full-length advance or promo. Noncommercial outlets (like college radio) prefer to be solicited with the complete full-length release. This can be accomplished by adding a quantity to your advance press run, or by setting aside a quantity of the finished CDs and "promo-izing" them (drilling holes in the bar code). Online radio outlets should be solicited with full-length copies as well.

Creation of a dedicated single. Commercial radio outlets (as well as some noncommercial Triple A and Americana outlets) prefer to receive a single (which always contains the album single, and perhaps some non-album tracks). Singles principally contain the following information:

- Sticker on the cover with radio contact info as well as ad date (usually)
- Radio promo contact on the inside tray card or insert
- Any quotes generated from advance press release mailing
- Track times listed for radio programmers
- Mention of full-length recording that single came from (for DJs to announce)
- Publishing info and legal lines
- "For Promotional Use Only" legal copy

Pre-Release Marketing to Retail

If you are working with a distributor, you will have a pretty fair idea of which independent retailers are interested in your music after the distributors' initial solicitation (which takes place less than two months out from street date). For stores that are particularly interested in the release, it makes sense to create some sort of "white label" sampler that can be played in store for a week or two prior to release to build up anticipation for the full-length. The formatting of these is not crucial; the goal is simply to get the music played and convert consumers that might happen to be shopping at the time the disc is played.

A retail promo sampler might contain the following:

- Packaged in an inexpensive slipcase
- Band logo on the cover
- Mention of upcoming record
- Track names

Pre-Release Marketing to Online Distributors

It currently takes online distributors (like TuneCore and CD Baby) six to eight weeks to have your music up on online stores like iTunes and Rhapsody. While these distributors submit your music pretty quickly, the online retailers themselves currently take an inordinate amount of time to make the music available. I expect that this process will be streamlined in the future, but for now, marketers need to plan at least eight weeks in advance in order to ensure digital store visibility around your street date. Online distributors appreciate a dedicated online-only, non-album track that they can pass onto the online retailers for promotional purposes. This track is due at the point which you upload your product.

Pre-Release Marketing to Blogs

Similar to online retails outlets, blogs appreciate a dedicated online-only track as well. Because the turnaround time with blogs is relatively instantaneous, marketing to blogs occurs much closer to street date than traditional press—in many cases only two to three weeks out from street date.

POST-RELEASE MARKETING RECAP

Although the majority of a music marketing campaign is put into place prior to a record's street date, there are a number of marketing support initiatives that artists should engage in after street date to ensure that the visibility of a new record continues as long as possible.

Touring

There's simply no better way to get visibility and build a community than getting out there and performing. Artists that don't tour have a tremendously difficult time keeping the marketing momentum going. Touring energizes every marketing segment, and in many cases, provides the link between marketing efforts and sales. Even if every independent retailer in the country is stocking your record, these will all be coming back as returns unless there is a reason for the local population to go in and buy it—and touring provides this reason, market by market.

Post-release marketing is heavily weighted to supporting a tour. Here are some of the considerations marketers should take into account when supporting a tour post record release:

Venue Support

A well-run marketing campaign will follow up on all tour dates by sending 11x17 posters announcing show dates to all venues a couple of weeks in advance.

Press

A publicity campaign is very clearly defined between long lead press and press designed to support a tour. Typically, publicists are hired for three-month campaigns in order to handle two months of long lead press, and then one month of market-by-market reviews and previews press (as well as any TV, NPR, or additional national press follow-up). For artists that have a heavier tour schedule, a publicity campaign can be expanded even further. Dailies and weeklies are targeted prior to the regional date and solicited with a tour-specific press release (with a local angle), phone call, and CD for top-tier regional pubs.

Radio

Throughout the course of a tour, a radio promoter will be working with individual stations to take advantage of any and all opportunities that the tour provides on a regional basis. Typical radio promotional opportunities include:

- In-studio performances (preferably those that are webcasted out to a larger audience, like LA's *Morning Becomes Eclectic* on KCRW, or WXPN's *World Café* program out of Philly)
- Ticket giveaways

- Larger support of a date (which might be a co-op expense with the venue and include a print ad component)

- Live performances at radio-sponsored shows or festivals

Retail

Touring opens up a number of opportunities at regional retail outlets. First, a tour provides a reason to increase the co-op spent at individual stores. In-store price and positioning, as well as visibility in local retail co-op print ads, makes more sense if the band is touring the market and folks are likely hearing about the band from more outlets than just the retailer. Touring also provides an incentive for the store to provide some additional in-store visibility, like flyers and posters that announce the upcoming date. In-store performances are also helpful in creating a larger buy-in with retailers, and also to move existing product off the shelves.

Online

A band's online visibility should be constant and current, whether working a record or not. But a tour provides a reason to go all out on your online marketing efforts. More eyes are likely to be on your site when you are touring, and proper positioning and updated information is key. The following items should be considered in an effective online marketing campaign, post release:

- an easy way to purchase the record

- tour dates front and center

- ticket giveaways to upcoming shows

- tour diaries/blogs

- video from recent performances

- exclusive webcast of live event

- tour merchandise readily available

- e-mails/texts to list about upcoming dates

- micro blogging while on tour (Twitter)

- any other creative community-building ideas you can think of!

PHASE II MARKETING: CAPITALIZING ON YOUR SUCCESS

There's really no way to know in advance which particular marketing "spark" will connect with your potential fans. There are countless paths that artists follow to find their way to success: the online community that propelled Arcade Fire, the independent retail support that Clap Your Hands Say Yeah received, and the constant touring that lead to the success of jam bands like Phish and the String Cheese Incident.

Over the course of following any marketing plan, you'll find things that have a tangible effect and move the efforts of the project forward, and things that do not connect at all. Once the plans you have put in place during the pre-release planning of the record have run their course, or something connects in a big way, many music marketers revise their original plans to take advantage of these successes. Remember, a music-marketing plan is a fluid, living document.

A phase II marketing plan looks at the successes that have occurred in the original plan, the events and activities that are upcoming, and possible ways to capitalize on these activities using the marketing segments that have worked so far. Please note: Phase II marketing plans are not for everybody, and should really only be put in place if there is momentum behind a release. There are many thousands of records released every year, and not all of them still have "legs" several months out from release. While it might be hard to call it a day once you see the momentum of a record decline, there's no point in continuing with a serious marketing spend when it is clear that the record's life cycle is over.

HERE IS A PHASE II MARKETING PLAN CREATED FOR THE BOSTON-BASED BAND, THE SLIP.

The Slip
Angels Come On Time

SALES and MARKETING PLAN
Phase II—begins mid September

We should all be proud of what we have done thus far for the Slip. The amount of press coverage, retail visibility, and SoundScan numbers so far (four times what their previous record did in the same time frame!) is really outstanding.

While we've seen some great select tour and festival dates from the band this summer, the following dates are confirmed for this fall:

8/23 Fri	Evolve, Antigonish, NS
8/25 Sun	Planet Pool, Halifax, NS
9/8 Sun	Tokyo, Japan
9/18 Wed	Northern Lights, Clifton Park, NY (Closest major market: ALBANY/TROY)
9/19 Thu	Anna's, Syracuse, NY
9/20 Fri	Milestones, Rochester, NY
9/22 Sun	UB Center for the Arts, Buffalo, NY
9/24 Tue	Rex Theatre, Pittsburgh, PA
9/27 Fri	Metro, Chicago, IL
9/28 Sat	University of Wisconsin, Madison, WI
9/29 Sun	Mississippi Nights, St. Louis, MO
10/2 Wed	Aggie Theater, Ft. Collins, CO (Closest major market: BOULDER/GREELEY)
10/3 Thu	Fox Theatre, Boulder, CO
10/4 Fri	Gothic Theatre, Englewood, CO
10/5 Sat	32 Bleu, Colorado Springs, CO
10/18 Fri	I-Spy, Seattle, WA
10/19 Sat	Fez Ballroom, Portland, OR
10/20 Sun	Wild Duck Music Hall, Eugene, OR
10/22 Tue	Humboldt State University, Arcata, CA (Northern CA)
10/23 Wed	Great American Music Hall, San Francisco, CA
10/24 Thu	SOHO Santa Barbara, CA

November will see dates in the southwest, southeast, and northeast.

FOCUS GEOGRAPHIC MARKETS

Other than tour markets, we should continue to focus on Boston, Providence, New York City, San Francisco, Boulder, Chicago, Burlington, VT, Austin.

PRESS

We're planning a multipronged attack for Phase II of The Slip press campaign:

- Regional press has been really strong for us. The fall dates see the band play markets that we have not had the opportunity to address yet in full force, and seeing the band is believing. We'll seek feature coverage while on tour with top regional outlets, with a special focus on the target markets of San Francisco, Boulder/Denver, and Austin.

- Target college publications. We'll service the record to hit when kids are getting back to school, and when we are going for college radio ads. We'll service the record with the color postcards (updated tour info stickered on back) and a press quote sheet.

- We're cross-referencing our original press list with the updated "jam friendly" press writers we've received from the Phish organization. Any writers we may have missed will be serviced.

- Continued pressure on national media outlets (*Downbeat* being at the top of the pile).

New reviews just confirmed in:

- *Bass Player Magazine*, October issue (out in September)

- *Modern Drummer Magazine*, December issue (out in October)

RADIO

We've had some limited success with our jam show servicing (most notably specialty airplay on WRAS in Atlanta, GA; KPFA in Berkeley, CA; and KEXP in Seattle, WA), but the goal is to really blow this record up at college. We'll definitely make the Phish connection known where it helps (recorded at Phish's barn, tour with Page McConnell's band Vida Blue), but we should also present this to college radio as a band that has extreme merits on its own, selling out theaters (1050 paid) in Providence, Japan plays, various successes at summer festivals (High Sierra), constant touring. More than likely, the band is playing near many of the schools where we are looking for adds.

Phase II radio plan:

- We're servicing 350 records to college radio in early September for a September 17th add date.

- We are running two half-page CMJ ads, which street 8/30 and 9/13, split with Pork Tornado.

- We'll get the band in studios where it makes sense along the tour route. They'll also do interviews, etc.

- We have signed CDs available for giveaways.

CMJ Festival

The band will be performing at Tobacco Road in Manhattan on Saturday night, November 2, at 11:00 PM (time subject to change, tbd this week). We'll distribute tour postcards with updated tour dates through 12/31 @ the merch booth. We are also looking for some cool ideas for merch or to tie in label profile stuff (Zappa, Pork Tornado are streeting a few weeks earlier). This is the first time the band has played CMJ; we need to be sure that we get key supportive music directors and program directors out to this show.

RETAIL

Great show so far at retail. The ship and scan numbers for a band that has had hardly any national retail support in the past is amazing.

We've made additional 4-track samplers, which we'll be servicing to key retailers along the tour route. We'll also cross promote the Slip record to retailers who are along the extensive Pork Tornado tour route in October.

We are all working together here. If our radio indie makes some noise at a particular college radio station, we should investigate retailers near the campus. We'll take these leads as they come.

Focus tour markets and retailers:

- Buffalo: Home of the Hits, New World Record.
- Chicago: Music Warehouse, Borders, Crow's Nest, Rolling Stone, Reckless, Rock Records, Dr. Wax, Record Emporium, See Hear, Virgin (will work with Ian to do bag stuffers here).
- Madison, WI: Borders, B-Side, Mad City Music, Strictly Discs.
- Boulder: Albums on the Hill, CD Cellar, 3 Wherehouses.
- Seattle: Easy Street, Rock Memories, Borders, and others.
- Portland: Ozone, Ozone UK (new), Music Millennium, Borders, Reverb, Tower, Wherehouse.
- San Francisco: Amoeba, Hear Music, Rasputin, Streetlight.

We're working with The Fox Theater in Boulder. *Get Me With Fuji* will be on a sampler of fall artists that are playing at the theatre. They're producing 7,500 samplers, which would be distributed to Boulder/Denver retailers as well as the theater itself. Retailers included are: Twist and Shout, Barts, Albums on the Hill, Wherehouse/Denver.

COLLEGE INTERACTIVE CAMPAIGN

We're targeting four markets where the Slip have a solid fan base: Burlington, VT, Boston, Providence, and Western MA for an interactive campaign. The idea is for all cylinders to be firing at once: at the same point that we are getting adds at college radio, reviews in college publications, and kids walking into college retailers, we'd also like to be having some Internet presence with the college kids, and a way to collect names of these kids we are marketing to. The thought is to work with pizza parlors that supply the colleges in these target markets, and get them some burned 4-tracks as incentive to hand out flyers which are a call to action: go to Rykodisc.com and sign up to win a hollow body Guild guitar signed by the band, as well as hear live unreleased music. The kids will need to enter their e-mail address to enter.

We called the schools listed below, and the targeted pizza parlors to work with:

UVM/Burlington: Manhattan Pizza & Public

URI/Providence: Kingston Pizza, D.P. Dough, Ronzio (on campus)

UMass/Western MA: Bruno's

BU/Boston: Anthony's

Brown/Providence: Antonios, Ronzio (also on campus)

MATERIALS

- 11x17 retail/tour posters
- White Label 4-track samplers
- postcards with key album art

Summary

In this final chapter, we looked at how to properly time your marketing plan. Like most anything in life, advance planning is crucial to success. Pre-release marketing should be considered for all the key areas in your marketing plan (retail, press, radio, online, tour) as well as packaging and merchandising elements. It's also important to note that the promotional items you send out to different marketing outlets require slightly different formatting and information. Finally, we recapped what marketing should be happening post-release date, and when/how you should consider capitalizing on your success with a phase II marketing campaign.

Workshop

Based on the information presented throughout this book and your responses from the end-of-chapter workshops, draft an outline for a regional or national marketing plan. Include the key timing elements we discussed in this chapter. As an example, if press is a component of your plan, when will you start your campaign? If you are hiring a press indie, when will this happen and when will they start? If you are working radio, when will you begin your campaign? Plan ahead based on a 20-week timeline.

Conclusion

This book provides a starting point for your music marketing efforts, the details on how to move ahead based on your unique situation, and information on how to take the tips and techniques contained within and formulate them into a plan for marketing success. But with any learning material, and particularly with any *music business* related learning material, it's key to keep up to date with the important changes that might affect your plan.

The record and music business is currently in the midst of a major sea change, with new artist service-related companies and other online marketing opportunities popping up practically every day. While this book provides evergreen segments and ideas that all music marketers must be aware of, I strongly suggest that you stay current with the evolving marketing trends by keeping up with online industry blogs and Web sites.

I teach this subject in an online course that I created for www.berkleemusic.com, the online continuing education division of Berklee College of Music. *Music Marketing: Press, Promotion, Distribution, and Retail* is a twelve-week course where students have direct contact with their instructor (usually me), as well as other like-minded students from around the world. It's a fascinating experience, and students not only learn the most current up-to-date marketing techniques from me directly in weekly chat sessions, but they also learn from other students that are in the midst of marketing their own music. Berkleemusic also offers a growing catalog of over a dozen other online music business courses, taught by Berklee instructors and top industry experts. It's worth checking out!

The site www.artistshousemusic.org is a free online musicians resource that hosts video interviews with industry luminaries, including Lawrence Lessig, Don Passman, Chris Blackwell, Jimmy Iovine, and hundreds more. I would also suggest reading or subscribing to RSS feeds from www.hypebot.com, www.futureofmusicbook.com, and Terry McBride's blog: www.nettwerk.com/terrysblog.

Lastly, you can keep up with me at my blog *Music Business and Trend Mongering*, here: mikeking.berkleemusicblogs.com. You can also follow me on Twitter at www.twitter.com/atomzooey.

I sincerely wish you all the best with your music marketing efforts and hope our paths cross in the future.

—Mike King

About the Author

Mike King is the associate director of marketing at Berkleemusic, the online continuing education division of Berklee College of Music. Prior to working at Berklee, Mike was the marketing/product manager at Rykodisc, where he oversaw marketing efforts for label artists, including Mickey Hart, Jeb Loy Nichols, Morphine, Jess Klein, Voices on the Verge, Bill Hicks, the Slip, Pork Tornado (Phish), Kelly Joe Phelps, and Frank Zappa's estate. He also handled copyright administration for a number of active and catalog artists at Rounder Records. Mike has been a regular contributor to *Making Music* magazine and *American Songwriter*, and has been quoted in the *Boston Globe*, the *Chicago Tribune*, and *Muso*. Mike consults for local artists and plays bass and guitar in the Boston-based collective the P. James Magic Show.

Index

A

AAC format, 36
Absolutely Kosher, 55
Active Rock, 158–59
ADA, 46, 60
ad-supported retail model, 40
Adult Album Alternative radio format, 159, 161
Adult Contemporary radio format, 159
advertising, 111–25
    campaign timing, 123–24
    catalog ads and one-sheets, 67–68
    components of effective, 121–23
    concision in, 123
    consumer print ads, 112–14
    co-op print ads, 66–67
    in marketing plan, 11
    online, 118–21
    phase-2 campaigns, 124
    print options, 112–17
    radio/television, 117–18
    sales spikes and, 118
    tagging retailers in, 123
    tailoring, 117
    timeline for, 192
    trade print ads, 115
AEC (Alliance Entertainment Corporation), 70
AIFF files, 35
AIMS (Association of Independent Media Stores), 63, 75, 77
Album Oriented Rock radio format, 163, 166
Amazon.com
    CDs on, 69
    MP3 store, 37, 41–42, 51, 54
    pricing model, 46
American Songwriter, 115

Americana radio format, 159, 161
Amie Street, 54
Anastasio, Trey, 37
Anderson, Chris, 40
Antibalas, 55
Apple Lossless format, 36
Arbitron, 158
Arcade Fire, 198
Aron's, 73
Arthur, Joseph, 90
artist/album description, in marketing plan, 9, 12
artistshousemusic.org, 203
audience, defining your, 5–6

B

Baker, Cary, 143
Balter, Dave, 7–8
Bangs, Lester, 133
banner ads, online, 119–20, 122
barcodes. *See* UPC (Universal Product Code)
Barsuk, 56
Bartlett, Don, 101
Beck, 155
Beggars Banquet, 132
Beggars Group, 146–48
Berkleemusic, 203
Best Buy, 74, 76
Big Cartel, 31
Big Hassle, 143
big-box retailers, 14–15, 62, 73, 74–76, 78
Billboard, 115
bin cards, 10, 82
bio, 128
Bjork, 91
Black Keys, 143
blogs
    on home Web site, 90, 92
    newsletters, 120
    pre-release marketing, 195

as press outlets, 140–41, 147, 193
Blue Wave, 27
booking agent, 170–73, 174–75
Borders, 62
Boston Emissions, 158–59
bounce rate, 97
Bronfman, Edgar, Jr., 102
Brown, James, 169
budget, marketing, 16–17, 157, 190
Bush, Brandon, 23, 183–84
Buster, Prince, 34
"buzz," 127, 147, 193
BzzAgent, 7–8

C

Café Press, 30–31
Caroline, 46, 60
catalog advertisements, 67–68
CD Baby, 47–53
    charges, 48–49, 55
    Internet radio and, 164
    overview, 47
    pre-release marketing to, 195
    ringtones and, 103
    sales process, 47–48
    TuneCore compared with, 56
CD duplication, 27
cell phones, 102–4
charts, radio, 160
Chemical Brothers, the, 91
CIMS (Coalition of Independent Music Stores), 77
Cinram, 27
Clap Your Hands Say Yeah, 63, 198
Classical radio format, 160
Clear Channel, 158, 166
clippings, 129
club owners, 174
CMJ, 115, 155–56, 162
Coconuts, 76
Coldplay, 155

college interactive
    campaigns, 201
college radio stations,
    154–56, 157,
    160–61, 201
commercial radio, 151–52,
    153–54, 157–60, 194
commercial radio formats,
    159–60
compression, 34–35
Concerted Efforts booking
    agency, 172–73
Conqueroo, 143
consignment, 80
consumer print
    advertising, 112–14
contact information,
    organizing, 5
Contemporary Hit radio
    format, 159
contract rider, 170
co-op, 66–67
    one-stops and, 70
    print advertising, 115
    visibility, 82
cooperative promotion
    with other bands,
    177
copyright exploitation, 20
Corgan, Billy, 74–76
Costello, Elvis, 91
Country radio format, 159
cover art, 82–83, 190
cover letter, 129
cover songs as digital
    marketing
    technique, 51
Creative Commons, 92
Criminal Records, 63–64,
    67, 75–76, 78
Cross, David, 121
cross-collateralization, 22
Currier, Terry, 77

D
data mining, 6
Dave Matthews Band, 44
Decemberists, the, 24
Def Jam, 19
Diamond, Neil, 37
Digital Millennium
    Copyright Act
    (DMCA), 36–37
Digital Music Group, 55
digital music players,
    space considerations
    for, 36
digital music stores
    (DMSs), 47

digital service providers
    (DSPs), 47
Dim Mak, 56
Dimensional Associates,
    42
Dion, Celine, 37
disc jockey, 153
Diskfaktory.com, 27
distribution. *See also*
    categories below
    definition of, 33–34
    evolution of, 50
    in marketing plan, 10
    strategies, 28–32
    umbrella groups, 63
distribution, brick-and-
    mortar, 59–71
    communicating with,
    69–70
    co-op, 66–67
    details, 64–65
    independent artists
    and, 63
    independents, 60–61
    inventory and, 69, 118
    majors, 60
    marketing tools for,
    67–68
    need for, 62
    one-stops, 70
    process, 59–60
    staff organization, 61
distribution, digital, 33–57
    basics of, 33–38
    distributors, 46–57
    pre-release marketing,
    195
    retail models, 38–46
DJ Logic, 55
Dodd, Sir Coxsone, 33
Drake, Nick, 20–21
Dreamweaver program, 96
DRM (Digital Rights
    Management),
    36–37, 41, 43
Dubber, Andrew, 29
Dylan, Bob, 92–93, 95

E
E1 Distribution, 61
Edison Media Research,
    163, 164
Electronic Press Kit (EPK)
    market, 175
e-mail from retailers, 67
embed codes, 106
EMI, 60
eMusic, 42–43, 51, 54
end caps, 66

event organizers, 174
exchange rate, digital
    music sales and, 41

F
Facebook, 99–100, 101
Factory Merchandising,
    27, 31–32
FairPlay DRM technology,
    36
Famecast, 100
Fanbridge, 101
Fancorps.com, 92
Fanning, Shawn, 43, 44
fanzines, 112, 138–39
Feedburner, 99
fees, distribution, 64
festivals, 175
50 Cent, 20
file formats, 35–36
FileMaker, 5
FineTune, 164
Fishman, Jon, 12–16,
    180–81
fixed pay rate for
    downloads, 38–39,
    51
FLAC format, 36
Flickr, 101
Fontana, 46, 60
free goods, 67
free music as marketing
    tool, 8, 85
Frenchkiss, 56
Fundamental Music, 20
f.y.e., 76

G
geographic markets, in
    marketing plan, 9,
    13, 199–200
goals, marketing, 4,
    178–79
Google analytics program,
    97
Google reader, 98–99
grammar resources, 89
graphic designers, 82–83,
    122
graphics firms, 27
Grateful Dead, the, 8
GReeeeN, 102
GroupieTunes, 54
Guster, 21

H
headlines, ad, 121–22
Hicks, Bill, 121–22
Hinder, 104

hip-hop marketing, 19–20
Hives, the, 27
hoodies, 25
"hook," 141
Hot Rod magazine, 117
Hunter, Charlie, 55

I
Imeem, 106
iMovie, 106
In Ticketing, 31
independent promoters, 17
independent radio
      promoters, 152, 157,
      160–63, 196–97
INgrooves, 55
in-store performances, 81,
      181–82, 197
Internet. *See* online/
      Internet
interviews, tour, 178
IODA (Independent
      Online Distribution
      Alliance), 55
IRIS, 55
ISRC (International
      Standard Recording
      Code), 37
iTunes
   about, 41
   artist payment rate,
      41, 51
   DRM technology for, 36
   exclusive releases for,
      74, 141
   ISRC codes and, 37
   physical CDs and,
      52–53
   pre-release marketing,
      195
   pricing model, 46
   Radio, 164
   ringtones and, 103
   size of, 33
   TuneCore and, 54
Ivy Hill, 27

J
Jackson, Michael, 104
Jakprints, 27
Jamieson, Bob, 44, 166
Jay-Z, 20
Jazz radio format, 160
Jimmy Eat World, 27
Joe Pug, 101

K
Keenan, Maynard, 121
Koch, 61

Kolowrat, Sonya, 146–48
Korn Go Green, 134–35
Krug, Steve, 89

L
Lala, 54
LaLonde, Larry, 12–16
Last.fm, 164
Les Savy Fav, 56
Lessig, Lawrence, 92
Levin, Eric, 63–64, 75–76,
      77, 78
licensing, 20
licensing agreements,
      online fulfillment
      companies and, 31
liner notes, 190
listening posts, 66
Luna, 67

M
Madlib, 105
Magnet magazine, 115
mailing lists, 177
manufacturing costs for
      CDs, 65
marketing plan, effective,
      3–18. *See also*
      specific components
   audience and market
      definition in, 5–6
   big picture in, 3–4
   budgeting, 16–17
   components of, 9–11
   distribution's place
      in, 62
   in-store performances
      and, 81, 181–82
   integrated concept, 3
   keeping current, 203
   licensing in, 20
   phase II, 198–201
   post-release, 195–97
   pre-release, 187–95
   sample, 12–16, 198–201
   SoundScan in, 85–86
   tailoring, 17–18
   timeline, 189
   timing in, 187–202
   tour support, 196–97
Marshall, Bob, 111
Martin, Ricky, 37
Matador Records, 106–7
Mays, Lowry, 158
MC Lars, 134
MC5, 133
McBride, Terry, 203
McKenna, Lori, 135
Meloy, Colin, 24

Menomena, 56
merchandise sales, 19–32
   appropriate quantities,
      26–27
   artist as brand, 19–21
   do-it-yourself, 21–22
   essentials, 24–25
   by label, 22–23
   mechanics of, 21–23
   merchandisers and, 22
   nonessentials and bad
      ideas, 25–26
   plan for, 23–27
   at shows, 28–29
   strategies, 28–32
Merchsquad, 31–32
Merlis, Bob, 143
Merlis for Hire, 143
metadata, 37, 94–96
Metallica, 43
micro-blogging, 10, 90
minis, 115
mobile technology,
      marketing through,
      102–4
Mogulus, 106
Morphine, 123
Morrison, Travis, 141
Mozes, 104
MP3 format, 36
msgme.com, 103–4
MTV, 104, 107
music director, radio, 153,
      154
MySpace, 29, 52, 87,
      99–100, 101, 106
MyxerTones, 103

N
Nail, 61
Napster, 37, 43, 44
Nasty Little Man, 143
Navarre, 61
New Found Glory, 27
Newbury Comics, 74
newsletters, online, 120
niche marketing, 5, 50
Nielsen Broadcasting, 84
Ning, 100
Nirvana, 107
Nokia, 102
noncommercial radio,
      151–52, 154–57,
      160–61, 194
NPR, 69, 118, 136, 140,
      147
NYCD, 73

O
O.A.R., 63
obi, 83–84
Ocean Park Music Group, 20
Ogilvy, David, 121
one-sheets, 67–68, 157
one-stops, 70
online fulfillment/merch companies, 30–32
online/Internet
advertising, 118–21
contest sites, 100
digital distribution basics, 33–38
DRM and, 36–37
exchange rate on sales, 41
exclusive material for, 141
home Web site, 87–99
importance of, 87
marketing plan, 10, 15, 18
marketing tips, 51, 87–101
merchandise sales, 29–30
music distributors, 46–57, 195
music retail models, 38–46, 51
music retail outlets, 40–43, 45–46
music sales, 33–57
MySpace and, 87
offline results with online marketing, 101
pre-release marketing, 195
press kits, 132
radio, 152, 163–65
social networking sites, 87, 99–101, 164
street team resources, 92
tour promotion, 197
turnaround time for, 123
viral campaigns, 92–93
opening acts, 173
Orchard, the, 42, 55–56, 164
Other Music, 67, 79
OurStage, 100, 101
Outdoor Life, 117
over-the-air downloading, 102

P
Pandora, 164
"pass through" number, 116
Paste magazine, 113–14
payola, 151, 158
PayPal, 29
Pearl Jam, 21
per impression (CPM)
online ad pricing, 119–20
Peraino, Dan, 172–73
Performing Songwriter, 115, 117
permanent downloads as retail model, 38–39, 51
Perry, Lee Scratch, 33
Phish, 12–16, 21, 198
photos, 129, 148
Pinback, 55
pitch letter, sample, 142
Pitchforkmedia.com, 63–64, 119–20, 140–41
Planet Music, 76
Podcasts, 91
P.O.P., 68, 70, 82, 192
Pork Tornado, 180–81
posters, 10, 16, 24, 25, 192
post-release marketing, 195–97
pre-release marketing, 187–95
long lead, 190–91
moderate lead, 191–92
servicing key outlets, 193–95
short lead, 192–93
timeline, 189
press, in marketing plan, 9–10, 13–14, 193–94, 199–200
press kits, 127–33
common problems, 132–33
contents of, 128–29
digital *vs.* physical servicing, 132
electronic, 175
goal of, 127–28
press releases, 128, 130–31, 146
tour, 178, 180–81
press stories, 133–36
on tours, 177–78
Pretenders, the, 83–84
previews, press, 178
Price, Jeff, 54

Price Per Click (PPC)
online ad pricing, 120
Primus, 12–16
Prince, 85
print advertising, 112–17
options in, 112–15
researching, 115–17
tailoring, 117
turnaround time for, 123, 193–94
print press outlets, 136–40
Pro Merchandise, 31
pro rata share, 38–39
program director, radio, 153, 154
promo copies, 68, 70
Promonet, 55
promoters, 174
promotion, compared with publicity, 136
promotional merchandise
in marketing plan, 11, 192
publicists, independent, 17, 141–48
insider tips on, 144, 145
need for, 142, 147–48
qualities of, 143
relationship with, 143–44, 146–48
publicity, 127–49
importance of story in, 133–36
pitching tips, 139–40
press kit, 127–32
print outlets, 136–40
promotion *vs.*, 136
record release press *vs.* tour press, 140, 196
timing of, 190, 193–95
tour, 175–82
publishing companies, signing with, 20
"punk," 133

R
radio
advertising on, 117–18, 136
airplay charts, 160
campaign costs, 157
college stations, 154–56, 157, 160–61, 201
commercial, 151–52, 153–54, 157–60, 194
community/public, 156
future of, 166

independent promoters,
152, 157, 160–63
Internet, 152, 163–65
in marketing plan, 10,
14, 152–53, 156–58,
164–65, 200
noncommercial, 151–52,
154–57, 160–61, 194
pre-release marketing,
194
promotion on, 151–67
publicity on, 140, 147
satellite, 152, 165
station personnel,
153–54
tour marketing, 196–97
Radio and Records, 115
Radiohead, 121
Real Networks, 45–46
record labels
artist marketing plans,
4
communicating with, 69
distribution companies,
60–61
falling sales for, 33
merchandise sales by,
22–23
tour support from,
182–84
recordings
cover art and
packaging, 82–83,
190, 192, 193
do-it-yourself sales of,
24, 25
exclusive releases,
74–76
importance of physical
CDs, 52
in press kit, 128
pricing, 64, 73–74, 80,
82
selling on tours, 179
singles for radio play,
194
RED, 46, 60
Redeye Distribution, 61
Religious radio format, 159
Reprise label, 74
researching like-minded
artists, 6
retail stores, independent,
73–86
benefits of, 77
coalitions of, 77
competitive strategies,
78–79

consignment and
pricing ideas, 80
importance of, 76–78
in-store performances,
81, 181–82, 197
in marketing plan, 10,
14–15, 200–201
opportunities and
resources, 80–82
problems of, 73–76
tour promotion at, 179,
181–82, 197
returns reserves, 65
ReverbNation.com, 92,
100, 101
reviews, press, 178
Revolver, 61
Rhapsody, 37, 45–46, 51,
54, 195
Rhino Records, 73
Rhys, Gruff, 121
RIAA, 38, 43
Rich, Buddy, 169
ringtones, 102–3
road manager, 173–74
robots, 93
Rock radio format, 160
Rocky Votolato, 56
Rolling Stone, 112, 115,
133
Rolling Stones, the, 74
Ropeadope, 55
royalties, ISRC codes and,
37
RSS feeds, 98–99, 104
Ruben, Rick, 37
Run-DMC, 19
Ryko Distribution, 5, 61,
118, 121–22, 133
Rykodisc, 69, 83, 180–81,
190

S

Sacks, Carla, 143
Sacks and Co., 143
sales staff, radio, 154
Sandman, Mark, 123
satellite radio, 152, 165
search engine optimization
(SEO), 89, 93–96,
120–21
Simmons, Russell, 19
Sivers, Derek, 47, 50–53
Six Degrees, 55
ska, 33–34
Slip, the, 198–201
Smashing Pumpkins, the,
74–76

social networking sites
Internet radio and, 164
limitations of, 87
uses of, 99–100
Something Corporate, 27
SongVault.fm, 164
Sonicbids, 175
Sony Music
Entertainment/
BMG, 60
SoundScan, 6, 38, 84–86
Spanish radio format, 160
specialty show host, radio,
154
Specs, 76
spiders, 93
spinART, 54
spine caps (obi), 83–84
Stickam, 106
Sting, 28
Stinkweeds, 75
Stitt, King, 34
Stones Throw Records,
103, 105
Strawberries, 76
streaming audio as retail
model, 39–40, 51
street date, 188
street teams, 92, 176, 201
String Cheese Incident,
the, 198
subscription pay rate for
downloads, 38–39,
51
Sugarland, 23, 183–84
suggested retail list price
(SRLP), 64, 73–74
Super D, 70
Superdups.com, 27

T

Target, 73, 74
target demographic, in
marketing plan,
9, 116
television
advertising, 117–18
publicity, 140, 147
tethered download as
retail model, 39–40
Thrill Jockey, 103
"tipping point," 3
Top 40 radio format, 159
tour accountant, 173–74
tour manager, 170
touring, 169–84
booking agent, 170–73
booking gigs, 174–75
club owners, 174

colleges in, 201
event organizers, 174
festivals, 175
importance of, 169
itinerary, 129
key players, 170–75
label support, 182–83
in marketing plan, 11,
    198–99
opening acts, 173
post-release marketing
    and, 196–97
press promotion,
    177–79, 196
promoters, 174
radio promotion, 152,
    196–97
retail promotion,
    179–82
road manager, 173–74
tour accountant, 173–74
tour manager, 170
venue's help, 175–76
Web site updates on,
    177
Tower Records, 62
trade print advertising,
    115
Train, 23, 183–84
Trans World
    Entertainment, 76
T-shirts, 24, 25
TubeMogul, 106
TuneCore, 49, 54–55, 56,
    195
Twitter, 90, 101

U
umbrella distribution
    groups, 63
Umphrey's McGee, 101
"unique selling
    proposition" (USP),
    6, 18
Universal, 60
UPC (Universal Product
    Code), 38
Urban radio format, 160
U-Roy, 34
Ustream.tv, 101, 106
Utne Reader, 117

V
Venue's promotional
    support, 175–76,
    196
Verve label, 111
Very, 61
VH1, 104

video marketing, 10, 104–8
viral marketing
    compared with word-of-
        mouth, 7
    online/Internet, 92–93
    retail and, 179
    for tours, 176–77
    videos, 10, 105
Voeveo.com, 103
Voices on the Verge, 69,
    118

W
Waits, Tom, 121–22
wallpapers, 103
Wal-Mart, 62, 73, 74, 76
Warner Music Group,
    61, 83
WAV files, 35
WEA, 60
Web analytics tools, 94
Web site, home, 87–99
    blogs and micro-blogs,
        90, 92
    as community, 92
    content, 89–90
    contests on, 106
    grammar resources, 89
    links on, 96
    measuring traffic and
        marketing results,
        96–97
    RSS feed on, 98–99
    search engine
        optimization for,
        93–96
    tour information on,
        177, 197
    usability, 88–89, 91
    use of media on, 91–92
    video content, 106
Weiss, Chuck E., 130–31
Wenner, Jann, 133
Wherehouse, 76
Wimpy player, 92
WMA format, 36
word-of-mouth campaigns,
    7–8, 85, 193, 201
Wordtracker, 94

X
XCP technology, 37

Y
Yahoo Music, 164
YouTube, 104, 105, 106–7

Z
Zappa, Frank, 12–16, 111,
    112, 169
Zazzle, 30–31

Serious

about your **future** in the

music business?

If you're serious about a career in the music industry, you need more than talent. You need to know how to make your music work for you.

More Fine Publications from Berklee Press

VOICE

THE CONTEMPORARY SINGER
by Anne Peckham
50449438 Book/CD $24.95

VOCAL WORKOUTS FOR THE CONTEMPORARY SINGER
by Anne Peckham
50448044 Book/CD $24.95

SINGER'S HANDBOOK
by Anne Peckham
50448053 Book $9.95

TIPS FOR SINGERS
by Carolyn Wilkins
50449557 Book/CD Pack.............$19.95

BERKLEE PRACTICE METHOD

with additional volumes for six other instruments, plus a teacher's guide

GUITAR
by Larry Baione
50449426 Book/CD $14.95

KEYBOARD
by Paul Schmeling and Russell Hoffmann
50449428 Book/CD $14.95

BASS
by Rich Appleman and John Repucci
50449427 Book/CD $14.95

DRUM SET
by Casey Scheuerell and Ron Savage
50449429 Book/CD $14.95

KEYBOARD

BERKLEE JAZZ PIANO
by Ray Santisi
50448047 Book/CD $19.99

HAMMOND ORGAN COMPLETE
by Dave Limina
50449479 Book/CD $24.95

PIANO ESSENTIALS
by Ross Ramsay
50448046 Book/CD $24.95

SOLO JAZZ PIANO
by Neil Olmstead
50449444 Book/CD $39.95

FOR MORE INFORMATION,
SEE YOUR LOCAL MUSIC DEALER,
OR WRITE TO:

HAL•LEONARD®
CORPORATION
7777 W. BLUEMOUND RD. P.O. BOX 13819
MILWAUKEE, WISCONSIN 53213

IMPROVISATION SERIES

BLUES IMPROVISATION COMPLETE
by Jeff Harrington
50449486 B♭ Instruments $19.95
50449488 C Bass Instruments $19.95
50449425 C Treble Instruments ..$22.99
50449487 E♭ Instruments $19.95

A GUIDE TO JAZZ IMPROVISATION
by John LaPorta
50449439 C Instruments $19.95
50449441 B♭ Instruments $19.99
50449442 E♭ Instruments............$19.99
50449443 Bass Clef $19.99

GENERAL MUSIC

BEGINNING EAR TRAINING
by Gilson Schachnik
50449548 Book/CD......................$14.95

BERKLEE MUSIC THEORY – BOOK 1
by Paul Schmeling
50448043 Book/CD......................$24.95

BERKLEE MUSIC THEORY – BOOK 2
by Paul Schmeling
50448062 Book/CD......................$22.95

ESSENTIAL EAR TRAINING
by Steve Prosser
50449421 Book $16.95

MUSIC SMARTS
by Mr. Bonzai
edited by David Schwartz
50449591 Book $14.99

MUSICIAN'S YOGA
by Mia Olson
50449587 Book $14.99

THE NEW MUSIC THERAPIST'S HANDBOOK, SECOND EDITION
by Suzanne B. Hanser
50449424 Book $29.95

MUSIC TECHNOLOGY

MIX MASTERS
by Maureen Droney
50448023 Book $24.95

PRODUCING IN THE HOME STUDIO WITH PRO TOOLS – THIRD EDITION
by David Franz
50449544 Book/DVD-ROM $39.95

PRODUCING & MIXING CONTEMPORARY JAZZ
by Dan Moretti
50449554 Book/DVD-ROM $24.95

UNDERSTANDING AUDIO
by Daniel M. Thompson
50449456 Book $24.95

MUSIC BUSINESS

THE FUTURE OF MUSIC
by Dave Kusek & Gerd Leonhard
50448055 Book $16.95

HOW TO GET A JOB IN THE MUSIC INDUSTRY – 2ND EDITION
by Keith Hatschek
50449551 Book $27.95

MAKING MUSIC MAKE MONEY
by Eric Beall
50448009 Book $26.95

MUSIC MARKETING
by Mike King
50449588 Book $24.99

THE SELF-PROMOTING MUSICIAN – 2ND EDITION
by Peter Spellman
50449589 Book $24.95

SONGWRITING, COMPOSING, ARRANGING

COMPLETE GUIDE TO FILM SCORING
by Richard Davis
50449417 Book $24.95

JAZZ COMPOSITION
by Ted Pease
50448000 Book/CD Pack.............$39.95

MELODY IN SONGWRITING
by Jack Perricone
50449419 Book $24.95

MODERN JAZZ VOICINGS
by Ted Pease and Ken Pullig
50449485 Book/CD.....................$24.95

MUSIC NOTATION
by Mark McGrain
50449399 Book $24.95

MUSIC NOTATION
PREPARING SCORES AND PARTS
by Matthew Nicholl and Richard Grudzinski
50449540 Book $16.95

POPULAR LYRIC WRITING
by Andrea Stolpe
50449553 Book $14.95

THE SONGWRITER'S WORKSHOP: HARMONY
by Jimmy Kachulis
50449519 Book/CD $29.95

THE SONGWRITER'S WORKSHOP: MELODY
by Jimmy Kachulis
50449518 Book/CD Pack.............$24.95

SONGWRITING: ESSENTIAL GUIDE TO LYRIC FORM AND STRUCTURE
by Pat Pattison
50481582 Book $16.95

SONGWRITING: ESSENTIAL GUIDE TO RHYMING
by Pat Pattison
50481583 Book $14.95

Prices subject to change without notice.
Visit your local music dealer or bookstore, or go to **www.berkleepress.com**

0809